THE MAKING OF A PUBLIC RELATIONS MAN

JOHN W. HILL
Founder, Hill and Knowlton, Inc.

NTC Business Books
a division of *NTC Publishing Group* • Lincolnwood, Illinois USA

Library of Congress Cataloging-in-Publication Data
Hill, John W.
The making of a public relations man / John W. Hill.
p. cm.
Originally published: New York : David McKay Co., 1963.
Includes index.
1. Hill, John W. 2. Public relations consultants—United States-
-Biography. I. Title.
HM263.H53 1992 92-15217
659.2—dc20 CIP

Published in 1993 by NTC Business Books, a division of NTC
Publishing Group.
4255 West Touhy Avenue,
Lincolnwood (Chicago), Illinois 60646-1975, U.S.A.

Manufactured in the United States of America.

2 3 4 5 6 7 8 9 0 VP 9 8 7 6 5 4 3 2 1

Acknowledgments

In writing this book, I have had encouragement, advice, and assistance from many of my colleagues in Hill and Knowlton, Inc., including Bert C. Goss, John C. Mapes, Richard W. Darrow, Don Knowlton, James J. Cassidy, Dr. Albert L. Ayars, Robert K. Gray, Loet A. Velmans, and others. To all of them I am most grateful. My special thanks to Paul J. Boxell for his valuable contribution in consultation and particularly in helping develop the survey on the subject of "public interest."

Contents

Foreword

A "modest public relations man" sounds a bit of an oxymoron. Successive cadres of public relations practitioners never quite succeeded in their attempts to change public perceptions that equate PR with slick. John W. Hill, a thoughtful, deliberate, silently shy and self-effacing man, always belied that perception. He came across as the atypical PR-man. There was nothing flashy about him: he did not feel the need to impress others and he abhorred name-droppers. In the twenty-five years that I knew and worked with him, I never once saw him take credit for any of the innovations he brought to the world of public relations counseling. He always leaned over backwards to give the credit to others.

Within his firm, he exercised a quiet form of leadership. Instilling a spirit of teamwork, he rarely showed displeasure. In a soft voice he would patiently explain that in his firm there was no room for anyone with a "big-I-am" complex. He often displayed bright flashes of insight in the many issues clients brought to the firm. But in meetings with staff or clients he was usually the last to speak and would give his opinion in a dry and unpretentious manner. It was his personality as much as the success of Hill and Knowlton that made him a legend in his lifetime.

An innate curiosity and eagerness to learn something new each day helped build his firm. Hill was an excellent listener and in his quest for enlightenment he tried to gain an understanding of many diverse political and economic views. He never disowned his own conservative principles, but they never stopped him from surrounding himself with a circle of friends, many of whom held what he thought of as iconoclastic views. He viewed the monthly dinner discussions he hosted at his apartment as a method of maintaining a dialogue with "opinion leaders." His regular guests, such as Daniel Yankelovitch, analyst of social issues, and Bob Bartley, now editor of *The Wall Street Journal*, ranged the gamut from liberal Democrats to staunch right-wing Republicans. As a result, when he made the rounds of senior as well as junior staffers' offices, his questions and comments demonstrated the scope of his interest, the breadth of his knowledge, and the depth of his understanding.

Born in 1890 and raised in Indiana, Hill was a mid-Westerner of the old school. Starting from scratch, he built his business step by step to a position of undisputed leadership, which it maintained during his lifetime. By the time of his death in 1977, most of Hill and Knowlton's "firsts"—the new services the firm had pioneered—had become integrated elements of the public relations and public affairs profession.

Characteristically, in this autobiography, Hill downplays some of his experiences as merely a natural sequence of events. His modesty does not permit him to mark them as the significant achievements they were.

Hill's major accomplishment was the building of the world's first broad-service public relations counseling firm. This was achieved on the basis of a set of twin principles which are even more noteworthy today than they were in his time: integrity and sound judgement. They guided each of his pioneering efforts.

Of special significance among Hill's achievements was the establishment of Hill and Knowlton's government relations office in

Washington, D.C. at the end of World War II. The small nucleus he constructed grew into a huge industry. According to his concept of "public affairs," Hill hired and supervised people who gathered information from government, supplied lawmakers with facts, figures, views, and positions and then backed up these one-on-one presentations with the broad dissemination of information through the press and other channels.

In 1952, when Hill was 62 years old, he made his first visit to Europe. This led to another innovation: the establishment of Hill and Knowlton offices abroad. This new venture began in Europe in 1954 when Hill sent me to Paris to open a one-man branch. That slim beginning was followed by the opening of fully staffed offices in the major European business centers, an acquisition in Australia and South East Asia and the setting up of an office in Tokyo. After these initial breakthroughs the firm steadily continued its foreign expansion. Thus, Hill and Knowlton went oversees when the term "public relations" was either not or hardly known outside the United States. For the first time, Hill translated the concept of a multinational public relations company into reality. John Hill also oversaw the development and expansion of a financial relations division, another first which concentrated heavily on "investor relations"—a system of communications between corporate management and shareholders. In the decades immediately following World War II no one could foresee how this modest enterprise would burst into a frenzy of activities in the 1980s, the decade of the hostile takeover and the leveraged buy-out. Hill and Knowlton launched an environmental unit in 1967, about ten years before industry was ready to acknowledge publicly the important problems of air and water pollution. This unit subsequently tackled other health issues.

Naturally, not all of these ideas were initiated by John Hill personally. Quite often, the plan for a new specialization was put forward by another member of the firm. But John Hill was the final decision maker and since he owned nearly all of the firm's equity, he put his own money on the line. Hill was keen to see each job done well and to the satisfaction of the client. He took great personal pride in the firm, but received compliments with a scowl.

In managing the firm, Hill was also a pace setter. Again, what he practiced was way ahead of the rest of the PR profession and many other service industries. Three examples come to mind. In the early 1950s the firm had approximately 65 employees. Since clients paid fixed annual fees, Hill was at a loss to determine how staff productivity related to revenues and profitability. Price Waterhouse, the accounting firm, recommended a time billing system, which was a replica of its own. Hill accepted the plan lock, stock, and barrel and hired the Price Waterhouse team leader as his firm's first chief financial officer. The Hill and Knowlton billing procedure inevitably became the standard for the whole industry. My second example is of the Hill and Knowlton European Fellowship program which I helped design and operate in the early 1960s. Hill would have been proud, but not surprised, to know that all the Fellowship alumni developed successful careers at the firm or elsewhere. My third memory is of an after-dinner speech in which Hill addressed the wives of his staff. This event took place long before equal rights became an issue. Already in the early 1950s a woman vice president was the Hill and Knowlton speaker at a convention of steel industry executives.

Hill's hallmark was his concern for his staff. Although it is not unusual for the founder of a small firm to possess a paternalistic interest in employees, Hill's mixture of team-building and morale-enhancing measures were greatly admired. Hill and Knowlton's various compensation benefits for employees included a health insurance program which, at Hill's insistence, equalled the plans of the largest and best-managed companies in the country; a generous profit sharing plan; and a stock option scheme in which a substantial number of executives participated. The employee policies had a beneficial effect: the firm suffered minimal personnel turnover in a notoriously volatile industry. In his 70s, while still mentally and physically vigorous, Hill relinquished his ownership control and encouraged wide employee share ownership.

In his political views, Hill was a complex figure. As a young man in the Farm Belt he had adopted an ultra-conservative stance and, before World War II, had flirted with right-wing causes. He never lost his disdain for the New Deal Democrats. This was demonstrated years later when, despite his innate courtesy, he refused to doff his hat in passing the FDR statue in London's Grosvenor Square. He pulled his hat closer over his ears and could be heard to mutter "Yalta."

When I first met John Hill in 1952 he had barely recovered from the defeat of his personal friend Senator Robert Taft ("Mister Republican") by General Eisenhower in the fight for the Republican nomination. He expressed the hope that Taft would put some backbone into the old General. Shortly thereafter Hill's brand of patriotism became tinged with a large dose of internationalism. Studebaker (which went out of business in the mid-1960s) was located in South Bend, Indiana, and was one of the first Hill and Knowlton clients with whom we discussed Hill's plans for Europe. Paul Hoffman, Studebaker's chief executive, had served as the U.S. administrator of the Marshall Plan and, together with other middle-of-the-road Republicans, directed Hill away from his earlier myopic perspective.

Often, talking with John Hill meant accompanying him on his long walks. Each day he walked for two hours or more and continued to do so well into his eighties. A tall and lean figure, Hill was a frugal eater, holding to an undeviating diet of no breakfast, fruit and cottage cheese for lunch, and a light dinner of grilled fish with a glass of draft beer. His lifestyle preceded the recommendations of today's nutritionists by several decades.

From 1927, the year in which Hill founded the firm, until well into the 1960s, Hill and Knowlton sometimes faced competition. But it was a mild and gentlemanly rivalry—a far cry from the fierce battles to gain or keep a client which prevailed in the 1980s and 1990s. It had allowed the firm to adhere to policies which are hard to maintain in today's world. Hill had ruled out political clients, including his favorite Republican party. He liked a fight that would defend a business cause, but shied away from non-business issues. Similarly, he opposed the hustling for new accounts. There is no need to go after new business, he would preach, insisting that outstanding performance led to satisfied clients, who in turn would recommend the firm to others. John Hill created a unique corporate culture, marked by an unremitting striving for quality and pride in performance.

Beyond his professional accomplishments, John Hill stands out as an innovative pioneer and trendsetter, an intrepid risk taker and a man whose intuition made him a brilliant strategist. The combination of these qualities led to an often almost uncanny prophetic touch. In a management memo written about 1972, after he had given up his executive power, the founder of Hill and Knowlton argued in favor of his company being acquired by a "large and financially strong company." That happened much later and three years after Hill's death.

In sum, the essence of John W. Hill lies not in his skills, but in his sense of fairness and honesty. As he writes in this book: "Counseling on public relations calls for a variety of special experiences, abilities and qualifications. In my opinion the most important single element is integrity, which is a matter of character." That is quite a legacy to leave behind.

SHEFFIELD, MASSACHUSETTS
JULY, 1992

LOET A. VELMANS
CHAIRMAN (RETIRED),
HILL AND KNOWLTON

Preface

EARLY IN THIS BOOK, John Hill tells of an incident of more than thirty years ago. It concerns his relations with one of his early important clients, the head of a major industrial corporation, about whom the author says: "My first clash . . . came one day in connection with the release of quarterly earnings. He always had been eager to get these releases prominently used by the press as earnings kept going up, but, when this rising trend changed, he told me to withhold announcement of the unpleasant facts. I protested this as wrong and indefensible." The executive got the point and authorized the release.

More important, this simple incident is an elementary reflection of the philosophy and integrity of John W. Hill. Among other things it explains why I was not only willing but eager to write a preface to *The Making of a Public Relations Man.* While I have often disputed John Hill's political views, I have applauded his public relations tenets and practices. This essentially quiet man, throughout my experience with him, has been unwavering in fighting suppression and advocating forthrightness. If bad public relations resulted from a dubious policy of a company or an industry, he has been the first to insist upon going to the top and urging that the policy be reviewed.

I have seen John Hill decline an exceedingly lucrative new account because the would-be client impressed him as wanting to shade the truth in dealing with the public. I have seen him back his associates and subordinates completely in disputes with major clients over what was essentially right and decent. And I have seen him convert many a top management to his point of view—which is essentially: Be sure your policies are right and fair, then stand up on your hind feet and tell about them forthrightly and repeatedly. I am certain that some of the more enlightened and foresighted policies of American corporations and industrial associations have come into being because management decided to embark on a public relations program and listened seriously to John Hill's advice.

I worked for John Hill for a number of years, first as a consultant, then as an executive vice-president of his firm, and, after becoming a dean, as a part-time consultant on noncontroversial accounts. The connection was severed only when I became a part-time editor (of the *Columbia Journalism Review*, designed "to assess the performance of journalism in all its forms") and foresaw the possibility of at least mild conflicts of interest. It is characteristic of John Hill that he understood the need for such severance.

This book, in my opinion, should be read by any executive who is thinking of embarking on a public relations program or modifying his existing program, as well as by any young person who is thinking of entering the public relations field. It is the autobiographical story of one of the true pioneers in public relations, who has adhered to high standards and made a magnificent success in so doing. The book is packed with revealing incidents in that career. It is sprinkled with fascinating vignettes of personalities ranging from Margaret Bourke-White and Louis Seltzer to Tom Girdler, Ivy Lee, Cyrus Eaton, and Roland Harriman. More important, it reflects John Hill's philosophy, developed over the years. It deals in some detail with the basic question of just what "the public interest" is in relation to industrial policy. It reflects Mr. Hill's deep belief that public relations is not mere publicity and press-agentry but a broader management function requiring a foundation of integrity, a forthright and understandable presentation of facts, and, finally, policies that are "sound when viewed in the light of the public interest."

I happen to disagree with Mr. Hill on a number of political and economic points. I cannot, for example, share his views on what he calls "the welfare state," and "free-handed government spending." I can agree with him in many respects on "the economic illiteracy" of much of the American public. I do agree with him profoundly when he says: "To paint all business as the soul of perfection is just as silly as to smear all business for the misdeeds of a few. . . . Public relations has no mystical power to work miracles. What it achieves in any worthwhile sense must be based upon integrity, and on sound attitudes, policies, and actions at the very top level of management."

John Hill has become one of the true experts in his profession. This book, I believe, will prove to be an important force in the continuing improvement of that profession and in its service to enlightened management.

New York, New York
June 23, 1963

Edward W. Barrett, Dean
Graduate School of Journalism
Columbia University

1

Perspective on the Problems of Our Time

MANY people have acquired a curious collection of ideas about the nature and practice of public relations. I long since have ceased being surprised when a public relations man is referred to as a "slick press agent," a "hidden persuader," or a devious manipulator of "dummy fronts."

The truth, unfortunately, is that among the more than 40,000 people engaged in public relations in America, there are all too many who fall into these categories, just as there are too many pettifoggers in law and quacks in medicine. Public relations is a relatively new and uninhibited field and anyone, competent or not, can hang up a shingle.

But public relations, itself, is a recognized and constructive force in modern society. We can see it at work in the policies and actions of almost every organization, business and cause in America—from the White House on across the land.

In its modern sense, public relations was brought into being by the ever-increasing complexity of the economic, social, and political problems that have assailed the human race in the years since World War I. Its roots are fixed in the basic fact that public opinion, confused, obscure, and unpredictable as it may often seem, is the ultimate ruling force in the free world. A fundamental function of public relations is to help public opinion reach conclusions by providing it with facts and interpretation of facts.

During more than three and one-half decades of practice, my interest has covered all areas of public relations. However, the field of private enterprise has claimed my special effort and attention. That is not strange in view of the deep-rooted devotion I have for a system which, with all its faults, has created so many rich values for our country.

Notwithstanding its manifest contributions, private enterprise travels no easy road. It has enemies and detractors who would point to its frailties, close their eyes to its strengths, and clutter its path with obstacles. Only with the understanding and support of public opinion can it flourish and grow. To attain this is the main objective of public relations for private enterprise.

There are no short cuts to this goal. Achieving it requires a total and continuing effort, starting indisputably with management attitudes, policies, and actions that are deserving of public esteem. The next step can be, and usually is, communications; the working tool of public relations. Some people like to think that they can ignore this natural order and beguile the public with communications alone, even though these may have little basis in truth or facts. Any seeming success from such efforts can only be short-lived. Public relations has no power to create any lasting value where none exists.

If public opinion is the ultimate ruling power in the free world, then it follows that the profound social, political, and economic revolutions of the past thirty years have had the majority sanction of the people. Whatever is to come in the future must also have their approval.

Industry has adjusted to vast changes in recent decades. It has had to take in its stride heavy tax burdens, increasing government controls over the economy, and the conferring of monopoly power upon labor unions by grateful politicians, together with many other encroachments and harassments. Undoubtedly industry will be confronted with more changes, for we are living in a world of accelerated change. Many of us who today are traveling in jets while astronauts orbit the earth were born with a buggy whip in our hands. We are living in the midst of the greatest revolution humanity ever has known—the revolution of scientific advance. With each advance come solutions of old problems and the creation of swarms of new ones. For example, automation brings new life and hope to many businesses and adds, temporarily at least, to the nation's woes of unemployment.

We are living in a world at war—called "cold"—and in the midst of an arms race beyond belief. As long as a stalemate exists in this race, civilization presumably is safe. But were the scales to be tipped seriously against us, civilization might well be destroyed. With these vast and frightening uncertainties, alteration and innovation nationally and internationally are the order of the era. Every sensible industrialist knows and accepts these facts. He knows we are living in a new social and political climate.

But at the same time there are also institutions and principles that are enduring and timeless. There are certain economic verities that are permanent and changeless—just as true in the Space Age as in the days of the oxcart. One of these is that two and two make four. Another is that when income in business, in the family, or in government fails consistently to equal outgo, there is eventual insolvency. And a third is that the profit incentive and the individual's love of private property lie deep in the nature of men, stemming as they do from the law of self-preservation. A fourth is that no business or institution is self-guiding; a driver is needed at the wheel. A fifth is that to keep abreast of the times in plant modernization, a company needs both profits and the money of investors. It will not get the savings of investors if it has no profits.

When these and other simple truths are forgotten in these turbulent times by the people and their representatives in government, the economy suffers. Then there is the temptation to turn to such panaceas as free-handed government spending. Some regard this as the only sure way to get the economy into high gear and to keep it there. They forget that private business is the major means of livelihood for most of our people. From the people's energies and creative drives come the real spurs to the economy.

The fact remains that the staggering spending programs by government at all levels have had public approval and, in good measure, are in reply to public demands for services or handouts. It is as easy as it is ironical for people to forget that the only source of government money is from their own pockets through inflation or taxes, or both. Many localities that frown on big government budgets, smile when they get a few million for themselves. It is the cumulative sum of these "few million" that helps make the staggering total.

What is the responsibility of business in these fundamental issues? Some people have sought to make light of industry's concern with public service and economic education. They say it is enough for business management to make profits—that nothing else counts. No one can question the truth that industry's number-one job is profits. The company or industry that makes money and jobs surely contributes effectively to the prosperity and well-being of the community. Because of this obvious fact, some managements spend little company money—and that grudgingly—to promote better public understanding of their own operations or of our economic system. Their attitude is to "let George do it."

There is a serious flaw in this kind of thinking—the same type of flaw that impels the beleaguered ostrich to stick his head in the sand. In the final analysis, private business exists only under the franchise of public opinion. The public, over the years, already has encouraged and approved a steady take-over of management prerogatives by bureaucratic authority. One serious effect of some of this take-over has been the impairment of profits. This is jeopardizing the private capital investment that must be relied upon to stimulate and renew the dynamic energies of private enterprise wherein lie the strength of the nation. It surely is the obligation of business management, by means of its public relations facility, to defend and maintain such freedom of action as now remains. All of the elements making for profits are not confined to the cold columns of the balance sheet.

Of course, there are innumerable useful ways in which public relations serves private enterprise in addition to the broad front of economic education. The services of my firm to clients in important industries in America and in many foreign lands have been widely varied.

These activities extend to every aspect of industry where public goodwill may be affected or at stake. They cover numerous phases of corporate life from labor problems to antitrust suits, from a plain press release to a far-flung institutional advertising program, from work at the grass roots to appearances before congressional committees, from the promotion of products to counsel on corporate policy.

Fortunately in this country every man, whether he lives in the White House or at the crossroads, has the right to speak his piece, to present his case. Public relations as we know it could not exist in Soviet Russia or any Communist country. In those countries, there is room for only one voice —that of the ruling class barking out the party line.

In this country, public relations is used not only by government, labor unions, and business but by hundreds of other profit and non-profit groups and organizations. It functions in the dissemination of information and facts when non-controversial matters are involved. But when controversy exists, public relations may become the advocate before the bar of public opinion, seeking to win support through interpretation of facts and the power of persuasion.

Public relations in its controversial usage is sometimes dubbed "propaganda." Actually propaganda was a "good" word until brought into disrepute when Hitler and the Communists began to pollute the airways with their "Big Lies," and made it a "bad" word. In a public relations battle in a free country it is important that there be no lies. Different interpretation of the facts is possible, and each side is entitled to present its views, leaving it to public opinion to decide which to accept.

The purpose of public relations in its best sense is to inform and to keep minds open. The purpose of "propaganda" in the bad sense is to misinform and to keep minds closed.

Business managements have every reason and right to communicate regularly with all segments of the public whose support they seek; and more, to work for better understanding of the private enterprise system.

Too often, we must admit, managements stir themselves to do something about the problem—then grow bored or frustrated after one flurry and leave the field, and the public, open to the unrelenting efforts of their detractors and opponents. Just as other good management programs are consistent and long range, so must be the perspective on the public opinion problems of our time.

This viewpoint, widely accepted today, has not always been so well understood. Certainly it is a far cry from the atmosphere that prevailed in my early years when, as a young reporter, I was starting toward a career in a field that was then almost unknown.

2

How It All Began

I FREQUENTLY am asked how I happened to get into public relations. Like nearly all of the early practitioners, I came to public relations from journalism. This was a logical step because it was to improve relations with the press that these men first were employed.

I had decided very early in life, on the farm near Shelbyville, Indiana, where I was born, that I wanted to be a newspaperman. My opportunity came when I finished high school in 1909 and was hired as a reporter on the old *Shelbyville Republican* at the magnificent salary of $6 a week.

In about a year, I resigned to go to the *Democrat* at a small advance in salary.

My new boss was named John Day Deprez, a kind and genial man with great patience. He needed it with me, as could be surmised by his repeated admonition, "Accuracy, my boy, accuracy!" I would like to think that this advice was not in vain. Certainly it has been one of the guides by which I—and my eventual associates—have tried to work since.

My father was an alumnus of Wabash College and even

today I have close ties with that splendid institution, being a member of its Development Board. However, largely because of the course in journalism at Indiana University, I decided to go there. After the university I went to a reporter's job on the Akron (Ohio) *Beacon-Journal.* Congressman Charles Knight owned this paper and his son, Jack Knight—now a noted editor and publisher—was a college boy getting his first taste of newspapering as a cub reporter during summer vacations.

While in Akron I developed an idea for a miniature daily newspaper that I was anxious to try out in a large city, so I quit my job on the paper and went to Chicago. There I met a young man named Gordon Ingalls, whose grandfather John James Ingalls had served for eighteen years in the United States Senate from the state of Kansas. Gordon lived in Chicago with his mother, a wealthy widow. He was handsome, had a winning personality, and a taste for night life. He liked my idea and promised to finance it, which he did for a time.

Thereupon, in the spring of 1913, we launched a new paper, the *Chicago Daily Digest,* the first tabloid to see light of day in Chicago, or anywhere else that I knew of. I was circulation manager, publisher, editor, reporter, and rewrite man all rolled in one. Ingalls was angel and advertising manager. Our plan was to distribute the paper to high-class restaurants and hotel dining rooms.

All went well at the start. Many restaurants welcomed the idea of having a small paper, with sports results and latest news bulletins, to hand to guests along with the menu. Circulation was growing and demand for the paper was increasing, but the income from circulation was insufficient to keep the paper afloat. We were not getting enough advertising. A little probing revealed that my partner simply wasn't working. I was in no position to crack down on him, for the simple reason that he was the financial backer of the enterprise. But I feared the worst, and with reason; because one day he came to me and said his mother had cut off the supply of dollars for Chicago's newest daily. It seemed she had gone to her brother, an executive in the Lord and Thomas advertising agency, and his advice was to cut the *Chicago Daily Digest* adrift.

But I was not finished with publishing. I returned to Shelbyville and joined forces with a close friend, Irwin Harrison, who had given up the study of law for journalism. Our scheme was to publish a Sunday newspaper and distribute it free to every home. We started it in the early fall of 1913, and it went swimmingly through the holidays until the end of the January clearance sales, when advertising revenues slumped and publication was suspended. However, our success with our give-away Sunday paper attracted the attention of the owners of one of the two regular papers in the town, the *Daily Republican.* They offered us the opportunity to buy the *Republican* and pay for it out of profits. We were eager to make the deal but it struck a snag when the owners placed a ceiling on our drawing account of $10 a week each. We thought this figure incompatible with our editorial dignity and held out for $15 a week. The issue was never resolved, and since I needed a job I went back to Akron, where I stayed for some time working at various periods on the *Press* and the *Times,* both now extinct.

On the *Times* I met one of the most unusual characters I have ever known. A reporter, he had the fierce expression of an anarchist agitator and that is precisely what he was—momentarily. But it didn't last long and soon he turned to short story writing with great fervor. The result was that *Redbook* magazine in 1915 proclaimed him as America's greatest writing "find" of the year. His name was Ray Sprigle. As a reporter in Columbus, Ohio, he had unearthed the "scoop" that Sidney Porter (O. Henry) had served time in the penitentiary there.

We became fast friends and decided on a canoe trip from Akron to New Orleans. After many adventures we got almost to the Ohio River when I deserted and went to Cleveland to a reporter's job on the *News*. Sprigle went to Pittsburgh to a notable newspaper career. One of his achievements was a Pulitzer Prize for his stories on Justice Black's one-time membership in the Ku Klux Klan.

On the *Akron Press* I met a tall, gangling, slow-moving reporter from Amarillo, Texas, named Bascom Timmons. He had a disarming grin and a delicious sense of humor. I liked him immensely, and I was sorely tempted when later he urged me to go to China with him. He eventually went to Washington, where he became the confidant and biographer of Vice President Garner and built up a prosperous business in the Capital representing various newspapers around the country. He is the only working newspaper correspondent in history to have had his name placed in nomination for the vice presidency at a national political convention. The occasion was a brief hilarious interlude at the 1940 Democratic convention in Chicago. Henry A. Wallace got the job.

I shall never forget one incident some months after I arrived in Cleveland. One of the cub reporters on the paper was a short, skinny, blond youth of eighteen years. His blue eyes were clouded with worry and I wondered why. I shortly discovered the cause one morning when the city editor, Sam Anson, called out his name.

Anson was a redheaded, energetic Irishman and a brilliant and resourceful city editor. He beckoned the reporter to a window close to my desk and bluntly told him he was fired.

"Take my advice," he said, "and go into some other line of work. You'll never make a newspaperman."

The young reporter gasped and his eyes became sadder

than ever. "But Mr. Anson," he said, "you can't fire me. My wife is going to have a baby, and I've got to have a job."

Anson's Irish heart couldn't take this. The youth stayed on the job and proved resoundingly that he could become a newspaperman. Today he is the influential editor of the *Cleveland Press and News*, Louis B. Seltzer.

I stayed with the *News* for two years. My salary advanced steadily from $20 a week to $25 where it seemed to hit a ceiling, and I began to look around. Anson left as city editor and was succeeded by a tall, dark-haired copy reader, whose name was Al Corrigan. When I told Corrigan I had an offer to go to the Penton Publishing Company on a steel trade paper at $27.50 a week, he asked me to hold off a month or so and he would try to meet this figure. I considered the matter carefully and finally decided that $2.50 a week in the hand was better than in the offing.

Corrigan himself soon left the newspaper and became an executive of the Kudner Advertising Agency. Since he retired a few years ago from the Kudner Agency, he has been a valued consultant to my firm in New York.

I had lived an exciting life on the newspaper, covering a variety of assignments from murder cases to politics. One of my beats was city hall. My opposite number on the *Cleveland Press* was an exceedingly bright young Lithuanian, Otto Tolischus, who later became a noted foreign correspondent of *The New York Times* and is today a member of the editorial board of that paper.

When I went to work on *Daily Metal Trade*, I feared that a job on a trade paper would be a dull existence. But I was wrong. Given the title of "financial editor," I knew absolutely nothing about finance and virtually nothing about business and economics. I had had no college training or practical experience in these fields; so I had to begin an intensive course of reading on finance and business. Finally, by dint of burning enough midnight oil, by wading through stacks of books, journals, and newspaper financial pages, and by asking questions of many patient bankers and businessmen, I began to make a little headway.

Within three years, I was writing a signed column for my paper. In addition, nights and over weekends, I was writing copy for a syndicated monthly economic and business letter used by about forty banks from coast to coast.

It was in 1919 that I had the first faint brush with the field I was later to enter. As a steady reader of the monthly *Bulletin* issued by the National City Bank of New York, I became convinced that some Cleveland bank could profit by a letter covering Cleveland business. None of the banks I called on would give the idea any serious consideration. I was about to give up in despair when I decided to make one last try—The Cleveland Trust Company.

It developed that this institution wanted to widen its connections with businessmen in the area. My idea of a publication for distribution to company officials struck the bank people as a possible answer to their problem. Thus it came about that the *Cleveland Trust Business Bulletin* made its bow in January, 1920. For $50 a month, working weekends, I acted as the bank's economist, producing a four-page letter covering the state of finance and business in Cleveland and in the nation.

The reaction to the *Bulletin* was somewhat startling both to the bank and to me. The local newspapers took to it and the ex-city hall reporter had the thrill of seeing his comments on the business situation liberally quoted with attribution to a big bank.

Very shortly, letters of commendation began coming in from dozens of businessmen. The bank apparently felt the experiment was paying off and, in a few months, it decided to set up a real honest-to-goodness economics department.

I was offered the job of heading such a department at, to me, the fabulous salary of $5,600 a year. The offer was extremely tempting, but I secretly felt that the bank was overrating my qualifications for the job. This view was shared by a bright young officer of the bank who said to the president, "If you are going to hire an economist, why not get a real one." He proposed the name of Colonel (later General) Leonard P. Ayres, then head of the Russell Sage Foundation. The bank hired Ayres.

The young officer who had saved the day was Ralph Hayes, who had been assistant to Secretary of War Newton D. Baker during World War I. Hayes later came to New York where he now is the distinguished head of the New York Community Trust. I always have felt grateful to him for stepping into the breach.

When Colonel Ayres came to the bank, he, of course, took over as editor of the *Business Bulletin*. I continued for seven years as his consultant on the steel business at double the pay I had received for writing the whole letter. He made no change in the format of the publication, which had been devised by me with the expert assistance of William Feather, a rising young printer of Cleveland. In fact, today—forty-three years later—the *Bulletin* still is being issued, looking exactly as Feather and I designed it in 1920. As for the quality of the content, let us confess there have been decided changes that are all for the better.

Colonel Ayres was a shy and gentle, but quietly determined, man. His business forecasts in the *Bulletin* soon made him one of the country's foremost economists. I greatly prized my association with him, as I also did that with an able young economist who assisted him—Bradford B. Smith, now economist of the United States Steel Corporation. In his office at 71 Broadway, he has a complete file of the *Bulletin* including the first twelve issues representing my handiwork.

My experience with the *Bulletin* had an indirect but important bearing upon my future course.

The Newspaper Enterprise Association obtained my name from the bank and engaged me to write a weekly business column for syndication among its client newspapers throughout the country. I turned this out on weekends, also; "moonlighting" is the term for it now. Visions of becoming a great newspaper columnist buoyed me as I turned my weekends to the writing task. But the arrival of the 1921 depression cut back newspaper budgets, to say nothing of my visions, and my column expired after about a year.

During my tenure with the NEA, I came to know and admire various members of the regular NEA staff. For two of them, my admiration has grown steadily with the years—one is Peter Edson, now a well-known Washington columnist, and the other is Bruce Catton, the noted historian, whose Civil War books I devour avidly.

I was depressed by the loss of the column and began to wonder what I could do to salvage or replace it. I thought of Eric Hopwood, editor of the *Cleveland Plain Dealer*, who some years before had offered me a job as the economics editorial writer for his paper. I asked if he would like to take on my column, and he agreed. The *Plain Dealer* ran the column for some five or six years, during which it served to get my name before the business community in Cleveland. This was to be of great value to me when I hung up my shingle later on.

I was able to show the gratitude I felt for Mr. Hopwood some twenty years later when, as public relations counsel for Republic Steel, I employed his young son, Henry Hopwood, as an assistant on the account. This proved a good choice all around. Today Henry Hopwood is Republic's director of public relations and a leading public relations man in the steel industry.

I opened my office in Cleveland in April, 1927. I thought I was going into "corporate publicity"—the term "public relations" was in scant use at that time.

I first became interested in the subject from reading a small book containing a collection of speeches by Ivy Lee. Lee had started his "publicity" business in 1904 after several years as a New York newspaper reporter. Along with most other newsmen, he had come to look with exasperation on corporate executives who ignored or spurned the press. He felt that if they would but tell their side of the story, their businesses would benefit from better public attitudes. He became known throughout the country for his work with his two most famous clients, John D. Rockefeller and The Pennsylvania Railroad, and he served many other important companies before his death in 1934.

Public relationships, he wrote, involved not simply "saying" but "*doing*"—not just talk, but action. His book abounded with straight-from-the-shoulder talk to business that seemed to make good sense. It kindled in me a determination to go into his kind of endeavor.

Although Ivy Lee considered himself in "publicity," he counseled on policy at the highest level of management and was unquestionably the father of the modern practice of public relations counseling. His work has been ably carried on by T. J. (Tommy) Ross. Another pioneer was Edward L. Bernays, who opened his office in New York in 1919 and, by his writings and speeches, has done much to call attention to public relations. Another was Pendleton Dudley, in whose garage in Chappaqua two young editors, DeWitt and Lila Acheson Wallace, lived and worked while they were getting their little publication, *Reader's Digest*, on its feet. Dudley started his business in 1909, but never adopted the term "public relations" until years later.

My determination to go into business also was stimulated

by the work I was doing in my full-time position on the steel trade paper. One of my jobs was to handle news about industrial companies, most of whose officials had no use for newspaper reporters and no desire to give out any news. Those who had news to report did it with incredible ineptitude.

It was clear to me then that most companies had need for help in the area of press relations. I set my course toward providing such help in Cleveland. But setting one's course was one thing and setting up in business without a single client was quite another. And I hadn't the faintest notion of how to go about getting a client.

The break came in the spring of 1927, when I was offered a job in the bond department of the Union Trust Company, Cleveland's largest bank. One of the top men in the bond department, Aims Coney, was a rising young banker whose somewhat brusque manner concealed a very warm and human individual. For some reason, he had taken an interest in me and we formed a friendship that has lasted for thirty-seven years. Coney had managed to engineer the bank into offering me a salary of $10,000 a year, but again I felt I was not cut out to be a banker and backed away.

In talking over the matter with Coney, I told him of my real ambition to publicize industry. He listened patiently and, when I had concluded, he told me quite matter-of-factly that I was crazy; that many of the companies in the Cleveland-Detroit area were broke and in hock with the banks; and that I certainly would go broke if I persisted in this foolish venture. As a practical matter, Coney was quite right. His views were correctly prophetic of the economic collapse of 1929 and, had I been wise enough to know what was coming, I never would have ventured forth.

As it was, I went home crushed and discouraged, but next

morning I had righted myself and my purpose was in full glow again.

About this time, a dramatic event profoundly affected my life. I had written an extended article for *Iron Trade Review*—now *Steel Magazine*—about the Corrigan-McKinney Steel Company of Cleveland. Several years prior to my article, there had been a bitter legal struggle for control between James Corrigan and his partner, Price McKinney. The decision went to McKinney. Corrigan and his wife went off to London, but in time he returned home and was able to purchase a certain block of stock that gave him control of the steel company. This purchase was financed by the Union Trust Company. My friend Coney had helped to work out the deal and a public stock offering was to be made by the bank.

Everyone was happy about the arrangement—everyone but McKinney. Corrigan went to see McKinney on the day before the stock issue was to be announced and told him that he was in the saddle; that he wanted McKinney to continue management of the company but under his, Corrigan's, control. McKinney was frightfully upset by the news. He went home and about ten o'clock that night shot himself.

Very late that night I received a telephone call. It was Coney. He told me in agitated tones what had happened. "Can you come down," he said, "and go with me to the papers? The editor of the *Plain Dealer* is calling me. It is terribly important that there be no implication that the steel company is in trouble."

I met him as soon as possible and together, armed with all the facts about the company, we went to the *Plain Dealer* and to the wire services. The result was that the suicide story did not reflect upon the company's financial position in the slightest degree, and the financing went off without a hitch.

This episode apparently convinced my banker friend that

perhaps there was something to my ideas, after all. In any event, Coney called me a few days later to say that he had spoken to John Sherwin, Sr., chairman of the bank, and that Mr. Sherwin wanted to see me at 3 P.M. that day.

I was there on the dot. Sherwin was easily the most powerful financier of that day in Cleveland. He was a large, handsome man with a shock of grey hair and keen blue eyes. He had a bluff, direct manner that was refreshing though sometimes disconcerting. He told me that, as an aftermath of the depression in 1920, some litigation involving him, Clarence Dillon, and the Goodyear Tire and Rubber Company was threatened. Opposing them was F. A. Seiberling, formerly head of Goodyear, who had retained, in addition to a battery of lawyers, a prominent New York publicity man, Carl Ackerman (later Dean of the Columbia Graduate School of Journalism). Mr. Sherwin thought this clearly spelled trouble and he asked if I thought I could be of help. I told him of my plan to set up an office and he asked me to come back in two days.

When I returned, Mr. Sherwin said the Union Trust Company had decided to retain "your syndicate" at $500 a month, if acceptable to me. In 1927, a retainer fee of $500 a month for a non-existent organization was not to be taken lightly. But it did not meet my expectations or requirements. I was desperate. Then I had an inspiration. In a display of unadulterated gall, I said I would accept his offer provided he would get me some additional clients. I knew of his influence in the councils of many important companies. Mr. Sherwin looked at me for a moment and then, without a word, called the president of a large Cleveland steel company, E. J. Kulas. To my astonishment, Mr. Sherwin told Kulas to hire me. The next day I saw Kulas—a rich, bouncing, high-living son of a Bohemian policeman—and the deal was made. I was in business and it was the greatest thrill of my life. I rented a small office and had some cards printed that said I was in the business of "corporate publicity."

My office was part of a "community" group of ten small cubbyholes and one secretary who served all of the tenants. Then for months I concentrated on learning all I could about about the technique and procedures of my new business.

During this period I did an institutional job for my steel client that pleased the company and also helped to start a young woman on the road to fame and fortune. One day a thin, dark-eyed, charming girl came to see me at my tiny office in Cleveland. She had with her a set of extraordinarily beautiful garden pictures that she spread on the floor. I was fascinated by these unusual photographs.

She told me her name was Margaret Bourke-White and that she had recently graduated from Cornell where she had done photography as a hobby. Now, in Cleveland on her own, she was trying to make a living with her camera. She was getting only $15 each for the garden pictures, and she wanted to do better. I told her if she could do as well taking pictures in industry as she had in the garden, she would be famous one day.

She became excited over the prospect, and I promised to see what I could do. My suggestion to my client, the Otis Steel Company, was that she take pictures in the plant that could be used in advertising and reproduced in a handsome booklet. The arrangement was made and the young photographer went to work with the intensity and enthusiasm of a zealot. She was absolutely fearless and insisted on climbing to dangerous and even forbidden positions in the plant in pursuit of a good shot. A few days after she started, I had a call from the night superintendent of the mill. He demanded that I keep "that girl out of the plant."

"She's crawling all over the place," he said, "and the men are stumbling around gawking up at her. Someone is going to get hurt, and besides they're not getting any work done."

I broke the news to the girl, and she was downcast. Then brightening, she said, "I'll handle it. I'll wear blue jeans." I went back to the superintendent, and he was agreeable. The blue jeans did the trick, and there was no more trouble. The girl took over 300 pictures that were developed in her small kitchen turned into a darkroom. When finally she was satisfied that she had something to show, I went to her apartment and we worked for hours sorting, discussing, and selecting. Out of this came about twenty pictures, each of which was a classic marking a new high point in industrial art. Mr. Kulas, the company president, liked the choice of pictures and agreed with my evaluation of $100 for each one used. He authorized me to proceed with the picture booklet.

The young woman began to feel that she needed a business manager, and she asked me if I would consider acting for her in this capacity. I felt that this role was out of my line, but I was so impressed with her work that I took a selection of her photographic prints with me on a trip to New York. I will never forget the gasps of amazement and admiration from some of the art directors of big ad agencies to whom I showed them.

I went all out in producing an institutional booklet for Otis Steel commensurate with the quality of the pictures. The booklet was distributed to a select group, with the result that firms began knocking at the door of the girl who had taken the pictures. She was given an important assignment by Chrysler, but her future was assured when Henry Luce saw the steel pictures and promptly employed her for his new magazine *Fortune*. Soon she had an elaborate studio high in the Chrysler Building in New York. It was not many years until Miss Bourke-White made good my prediction and became world famous as a photographer and writer. With her artistry, her charm, and her irresistible will to succeed, nothing could stop her—nothing until she was stricken by Parkinson's disease in 1952. But even her courageous fight against this disease has been a medical marvel. In her new book *Portrait of Myself*, Miss Bourke-White recalls the early steel pictures.

We have remained friends over the years. It was at a reception in her honor many years later that I met another woman of great ability. I remember the incident with rueful amusement. After arriving at the New York Overseas Press Club, I first saw Margaret Bourke-White in the company of Mr. and Mrs. Henry Luce in the library. We chatted for a time and then I moved on to talk with other guests. A short while later, I again came upon the trio standing in another room and began to reminisce with Henry Luce about the old days in the twenties when he and Britton Hadden brought their new publication to Cleveland to be printed by the Penton Publishing Company. Mr. Luce and Mr. Hadden alternated each month as business manager and editor.

The *Time* editorial sanctum was in the printing plant of the Penton Company. I was an editor of Penton's Iron Trade Review, and occasionally would drop in to discuss steel or other items with Mr. Luce or Mr. Hadden, depending on who was editor that particular month. This talk with Mr. Luce of the old days went on for a moment or two when suddenly Mrs. Clare Boothe Luce tapped me on the arm and indicated she wanted to speak with me privately. As I gave her my ear, I wondered what tidbit of confidential information this noted woman of letters and former ambassador to Italy wanted to give me. What she said was, "I'm terribly sorry, but I must tell you that you are holding up the reception line."

When I was retained by the Union Trust Company, I was forced—sadly—to sever my long-time association with the Cleveland Trust and Colonel Ayres.

During that first year in my tiny new office, I began to realize that my activities were destined to extend far beyond the important job of press relations. I was getting into other forms of communication. My steel company client asked me to take over the job of editing an employee publication. This put me into many problems of labor relations and communications. I conferred at regular intervals with the president and members of his top management, all of whom took me into their confidence.

I arranged a few press conferences and shall never forget the first of these. One of the reporters was a most likeable chap who had recently been assigned to business writing after years of covering horse racing. He knew nothing whatever about steel, but he was anxious to learn. Kulas himself had spent his life and made a fortune in another business and knew little about the technology of steel. So when the newsman asked him to explain the process of making steel he was stumped for an instant, then he replied:

"There's no trick at all to making steel. It's selling the damned stuff that's the problem."

My first clash on policy with Kulas came one day in connection with the release of quarterly earnings. He always had been eager to get these releases prominently used by the press, as earnings kept going up. But, when this rising trend changed, he told me to withhold announcement of the unpleasant facts. I protested this as wrong and indefensible. I said that a policy of releasing earnings only when they are good would utterly destroy any goodwill the company was trying to build up with the press and in the financial community. Kulas, a highly intelligent man, was quick to get the point and authorized the release.

One of the close advisers of the Otis Steel president was a prominent Cleveland lawyer, Frank Ginn, a picturesque figure with long flowing locks. Mr. Ginn always was friendly to me, although I had a secret feeling that he was none too happy about my relationship with some of his clients. My feeling was confirmed one day when I innocently asked him to help me get as an account a company of which he was a Board member. His response was that, "If any company that I am advising ever should consider your employment for what you choose to call public relations, I will oppose it."

This was rather a stiff blow to a budding young public relations man, but I think it was the general attitude of lawyers of that era. Mr. Ginn evidently felt that communications with the public were a legal responsibility and that he could provide all the advice and service any client might need; no specialist was required. Time has wrought a great change in that attitude. The present generation of corporation lawyers accepts public relations people without question. They are happy to work with us freely and in close cooperation whenever it serves the interests of the client to do so.

No new business came in to the new firm during the first few months. Then it began to pick up briskly. One reason, I suppose, was that I had no competition in Cleveland and another was that a word in my favor had been dropped here and there by my two clients. I had a terrific problem of expansion of office space and staff.

New accounts included The Austin Company, construction engineers; Pickands Mather, the great ore firm; Cyrus Eaton's Continental Shares; United Alloy Steel; Richman Brothers Company, clothes; and Standard Oil of Ohio. Although the Great Depression started in 1929, no important attrition affected my business until the bank closings in the spring of 1933.

The new accounts brought new problems but, best of all, new and stimulating acquaintances in the business world. One of these was the president of United Alloy Steel of Massillon, Ohio. His name was Ben Fairless who, years later, was to become an outstanding leader in the American steel industry. My first recollections of Ben Fairless are vivid. I drove to Massillon from Cleveland once each week. On my first trip I was taken by Jack Schlendorf, manager of sales, and Larry Hamaker, advertising director, into the president's office. There I was greeted with a warming smile and a firm handshake by a trim, ruddy-faced man, whose youthfulness surprised me. He was then about thirty-eight years old. I met Ben Fairless often after this for some years and worked with him closely again in the years before his death, after his retirement as chairman of United States Steel Corporation, when he was president of American Iron and Steel Institute.

Ben Fairless was a man who attracted wide and loyal friendships. He had a rare and shining quality of genuine sincerity that commanded deep respect.

He was born in Pigeon Run, Ohio, the son of a coal miner. His name was Benjamin F. Williams, but when he was two years old his mother was injured, and he was taken into the home of an uncle who later adopted him. His legal name became B. F. Fairless. He worked his way through high school and college by teaching and playing baseball and got his first job as an engineer helping to build the steel plant in Massillon, of which he was to become president. In 1930 he became executive vice president of the new Republic Steel, and in 1935 he joined United States Steel Corporation. But although he rose to great heights in American industry, Ben Fairless never lost the human touch with which he was imbued in the early years among the plain people of Pigeon Run.

Although as president of U.S. Steel he was widely known, he became a truly national figure overnight as the result of a fighting speech he made in Baltimore on April 21, 1950. He was due in the following week to testify before a hostile, headline-seeking congressional committee—the Subcommittee on the Study of Monopoly Power of the House Committee on the Judiciary. His speech was a courageous and ringing denunciation of the methods of business-baiters in Congress and the executive branch of the Government. It was also a sound and telling affirmation of the contributions of American private enterprise.

Public reaction was electric. In the press and by word of mouth, the speech was acclaimed across the country. The company for weeks was flooded with requests for copies of it. Nor was the impact felt any less in Washington. The usually abusive members of the investigating committee, on whom Mr. Fairless had turned the fire of public scorn, treated him with careful courtesy and respect throughout his appearance.

Assisting Mr. Fairless in drafting the speech had been an able new member of the company's public relations staff, Phelps H. Adams. For twenty-five years Adams had been Washington correspondent of the old *New York Sun*. He is now vice president, public relations, of U.S. Steel.

To get back to Cleveland in the twenties—among the names to be remembered during those years were the Van Sweringens. They were two brothers who got their start as real estate developers; their most famous project being the Shaker Heights area. Both were attractive young men, full of ambition and bursting with energy and drive. Neither was married. O. P., the older, was the dreamer, the empire builder. His brother, M. J., was warmer, less dour, and the salesman. The brothers had promised Shaker Heights property owners that there would be a rapid transit to downtown Cleveland. To make good on that promise they got financial backing for the purchase of the Nickel Plate Railroad that owned a right of way and was ideal for the rapid transit.

The Nickel Plate purchase turned out to be enormously profitable and the brothers, their ambitions fired by success in their new venture, lost no time in following this lead. The Nickel Plate was used as the basis of acquiring control of many other important railroad properties. These properties included the Chesapeake & Ohio, Pere Marquette, Erie, Wheeling & Lake Erie, Missouri Pacific, and others. One of the most fantastic railroad empires in the history of the country was created, but its financial structure was incredibly complex and it was inadequately financed. The depression of the thirties brought its collapse.

I was never retained by the Van Sweringens but always felt friendly to them because they were close to many of my clients, with the single exception of Cyrus Eaton, a rapidly rising financier.

I think that mutual ill will and distrust had long been simmering between the Van Sweringen group and Eaton. It was brought to the boiling point when Eaton, early in 1930, announced his intention to wage a proxy fight to prevent Bethlehem Steel from carrying out its plans to purchase The Youngstown Sheet & Tube. The powerful camps were lined up on opposing sides with the Van Sweringens, the Sherwins, and their friends in Cleveland and New York in all-out support of Bethlehem, while Eaton and his group were in opposition. The proxy battle that followed was one of the most bitter conflicts of the kind of this century.

Obviously, with important connections in both camps, my position was precarious. Powerful interests were clashing and the stakes were high, in addition to which tempers were inflamed and personalities were involved. I could easily have been crushed in the fight and before it was all over I thought I was going to be.

However, during the proxy contest I fortunately had no calls for service from the pro-Bethlehem forces in Cleveland —probably because the public relations was being handled in the East by Bethlehem. Eaton, however, called me into action at once, as I was retained by his Continental Shares. He asked me to undertake certain assignments in the preparation of materials, releases, and speeches.

Although Eaton had expressed confidence in winning the proxy fight, the final tally showed his shares to be in the minority and the merger was approved by the stockholders. But Eaton had no intention of accepting this verdict. His restless acquisitive mind was bent on achieving a great steel empire in the Middle West, and he wanted Youngstown Sheet & Tube as a part of it. I heard rumors that he was planning court action to stop the merger. I was greatly alarmed by this. I felt that, with a depression getting under way, to prolong this bitter industrial war would be a bad thing for the country as well as for me. I strongly advised against it. But the Eaton camp filed the suit.

After a long and costly court trial in Youngstown, Eaton succeeded in getting an injunction against the merger. The case was appealed, and a higher court ruled about two years later that the injunction should not have been granted. By that time, however, the onset of the depression had made the merger less attractive, and Bethlehem had decided not to go ahead with it.

But Eugene G. Grace, Bethlehem's president, did not forget the potential advantages of a merger with Youngstown. In the mid-fifties, Bethlehem tried to effect the consolidation once again, only to have the second effort opposed by a Republican Department of Justice. A federal court ruled against the merger.

It has been my fate to be involved in two of the most important proxy contests in the nation's financial history. The second, thirty-one years after the Bethlehem-Youngstown struggle, was the contest for control of Alleghany Corporation, won by our clients, the Murchison brothers of Texas.

Eaton, as well as the Van Sweringens, suffered heavy losses

in the Great Depression. However, he made a remarkable comeback through his Cleveland securities house, Otis and Co., and is again today a man of great financial power. He is best known to the public as friend and confidant of Nikita Khrushchev.

One day, shortly after the proxy fight was over but before the court contest was started, my original sponsor, John Sherwin, Sr., sent for me. When I arrived in his office, he came to the point at once. He had heard, he said, that I had worked for Eaton in the proxy fight. I told him that was true. "Well," he said, "we have nothing against you but you can't work for Eaton and for any of our friends at the same time. You're an innocent party in this fight and no one will criticize you if you feel it is more advantageous to stay with Eaton. Make your choice and let me know tomorrow."

This ultimatum confronted me with a major crisis. Exactly one-half of my income was coming from Eaton's enemies and the other half from his friends. I went home to a sleepless night. The problem I struggled with during the night was how to placate Mr. Sherwin without sacrificing one-half of my income and destroying my organization.

By morning I thought I had the answer. I would go to my friend, John Sherwin, Jr., and ask him to intercede with his father. My proposal was that I would resign the Eaton Continental Share account as soon as I had completed a special research job then under way; that, meanwhile, I would take no further part in the Grace-Eaton merger struggle; and that I would be permitted to hold other Eaton accounts unrelated to the merger.

Young John Sherwin, as he was known, listened sympathetically and promised to talk to his father about the matter that day. The next day he told me my plan was acceptable. I always have been grateful for what the Sherwins, father and son, did for me. John Jr., unlike many another rich man's son, has devoted himself to useful activities and today heads the world's largest iron ore company and is a director of American Iron and Steel Institute.

The acceptance of my proposal was one of those happenings that in retrospect was another landmark in my career. Had it been rejected, my sense of loyalty to the Sherwins would have compelled me to resign a new steel company account that was to be of the utmost importance in the future development of my organization.

One fine spring day shortly before Mr. Sherwin called me in to see him, Russell Burwell, then president of Continental Shares, introduced me to a man with whom I was to be closely associated for eighteen years. His name was Tom Girdler. He was a man of medium height, keen-eyed and handsome. He was also sharp-witted, fearless, decisive and ruthless. If you were looking for a rugged individualist, here was the genuine article, possessing all the ingredients necessary for the nationally controversial figure he was to become.

Girdler had a penchant for direct and picturesque language, and he was famous for his tangy stories. He must have had access to the source of all such stories, because I never heard anyone tell one he didn't know.

He was a native of southern Indiana where his father owned and ran a small cement mill. Tom Girdler was always proud of his ancestry. His paternal grandfather had been a Yankee ship captain and his father had fought in the Civil War. "Good or bad, every fiber in me is American," he once wrote.

Young Tom attended Lehigh University to study engineering, for which he had great aptitude. During the summer before his senior year, he took charge of the cement mill while his father went off on a long-delayed vacation trip; and the son ran the operation so successfully that his father, when he returned, was almost as jealous as he was proud. But cement milling was not what Girdler wanted to do. After his graduation, he worked briefly for a forge company and then took a job, at $1,000 a year, with the Oliver Iron & Steel Company in Pittsburgh. Starting as a departmental foreman, he was soon put to the test by a tough young worker in his section. The man had sauntered off the job several minutes before quitting time. Girdler ordered him back. Hot words flared into a bitter fight that ended when Girdler knocked his bigger opponent out cold. There could have been no more typical way for the Girdler career in steel to begin.

In time he became president of the Jones & Laughlin Steel Corporation, from which he was lured by Cyrus Eaton in 1930 to head the new Republic Steel Corporation. Later, however, there was a break between Eaton and Girdler.

When I met him, Girdler was putting his organization together and charting his course. With him from J & L he had brought Rufus (Jack) Wysor and a tall, energetic—and also colorful—steel operating man, Charles M. White. Ben Fairless came in from United Alloy and these three constituted Girdler's "first team" of executives until 1935 when Fairless became president of Carnegie Steel. White later became president of Republic and then chairman, and one of the nation's most articulate industrial leaders.

Girdler retained me at our first meeting. Working with him and his group gave me a new vision of the dimensions of public relations. It was my largest account up to that time. My small staff and I were kept on the run serving Republic and six other accounts.

As the Depression deepened in 1933, my clients reduced the salaries of executives up to 20 per cent and my fee by the same amount—that is, all but one, Standard Oil of Ohio. This company had become one of my early clients in 1928, the result of friendship with the assistant to the president, a young man named Sidney Swensrud, who before his retirement was to become chairman of Gulf Oil. Sidney introduced me to the president, William T. Holliday, a former corporation lawyer, who came as near to my idea of an industrial statesman as anyone I ever have known. The fact that there was silence about the fee from that quarter worried me. I decided to make the suggestion myself before I was cut off altogether.

When I went to see Mr. Holliday, he laughed and said there was no thought in his mind of reducing my fee. Then he startled me by saying that my fees were too low anyway; that my whole basis of charges was wrong. I should have fixed per diem rates, he said, like lawyers. The day was to come when I would do just this. However, it was not right away because, like other practitioners seeking to establish their worth, I was hesitant to insist on a new basis for client pay. But, later on, when we had built a considerable staff, we put all the firm's affairs on a business footing, with standard fees and staff time charges applying to all clients alike.

And Mr. Holliday was right—we found that our clients preferred a system whereby they paid for the services of our individual staff members only to the extent that they made use of these services. This, as I will note in a later chapter, has been the basis of our charges ever since.

Shortly after that 1933 conversation, Mr. Holliday called me in to discuss the possibility of a full-page ad in Ohio papers to allay the feeling of panic and to bolster confidence. It was during the 100 days after Roosevelt's inauguration, and Holliday wanted to tell the people to be calm and to give the new President a chance. Since this was to be an institutional and public service ad, he said he wanted my help on it rather than that of the advertising agency that was busy trying to sell gasoline. We worked together for several days refining this ad and, when it was run, it received much favorable reaction.

Mr. Holliday and I became good friends. I consulted with him often and carried out various assignments for him as long as he lived. One of the most unforgettable of these was to talk with John D. Rockefeller, Jr., in connection with an anniversary celebration of Sohio, successor to the company founded by his father in Cleveland in 1870. Mr. Rockefeller graciously received me in his office in Rockefeller Center and quickly gave me the information I wanted. Then, having started reminiscing about his father, he warmed to his subject with animation, and what I thought was to be a twenty-minute interview extended to an hour and a half. He told me many fascinating stories about the elder Rockefeller, and I shall always remember with what deep reverence he spoke of his father.

When the banks were closed down in March, 1933, my first client, The Union Trust Company, was a permanent victim.

Many of the bank employees were out of work. One of them was Don Knowlton, director of advertising and public relations for the bank. We had worked closely together, and I invited him to join me in a partnership, which he did. The firm became Hill and Knowlton.

I had first met Knowlton some time after I had been retained by the bank, when he was assistant director of advertising and publicity. He later became director and, when we met in the bank lobby one day, he said, "I'm going to recommend the continuance of your work, but at a reduced fee."

"Why is that?" I asked.

"Very simple," he replied. "You are giving only part time to the bank for a fee of $500 a month, and this exceeds my full-time salary. This has got to be adjusted."

I told him he was quite right about an adjustment being needed, but the way to do it was by an increase in his salary, not by cutting my fee. Knowlton saw the light immediately.

Next morning he went to the bank management and demanded a substantial increase for his new job, and got it.

During the bank closings of 1933 there occurred an incident that I here report because it has a bearing upon one of the underlying principles of public relations.

I had learned, by practice supported by instinct, that newspapers would accept and print stories about client companies only if they felt assured that the stories were true. In short, the facts presented had to be accurate and subject to substantiation. The result was that my office had worked hard to build up from the very start a reputation for reliability.

A test of this reputation came in the spring of 1933. All the banks in Ohio had been closed down, by decree of the Governor of the state. Their accounts were frozen. They were then reopened for the handling of new "segregated" accounts, for business had to be continued to be transacted and payrolls had to be met. Firms and individuals dug up money they had stashed away, or had on deposit in banks still open in other parts of the country, and put such funds in these "segregated" accounts.

Then—five days after the Governor had closed the Ohio banks—President Roosevelt issued an order closing all the banks in the country.

Maurice Hanning, a close friend and attorney for the Standard Oil Company of Ohio, Don Knowlton, and I were sitting in Maurice's office that tense evening, when a phone call came through for me from the *Cleveland Plain Dealer*. It was the city editor.

"Does the President's order just continue to freeze the accounts already frozen by the Governor's order," he asked, "or does it also include the new segregated accounts? If the latter, there will be hell to pay. But nobody knows. We can't find out. We're holding the presses. Is there anything you can do?"

"I'll try," I told him.

I phoned J. R. Kraus, vice chairman of the suddenly defunct Union Trust Company. He phoned Senator Bulkley. Senator Bulkley phoned President Roosevelt. Back to me, by the same route, came the word:

"The President's order does *not* include the segregated accounts."

Knowlton and I took a quick cab to the *Plain Dealer.* The city editor was waiting for us. I told him the answer. "Start the presses!" he ordered.

Then he explained to me that all the papers in the state, and all the wire services, had likewise been waiting for the "word"—which they would now get, pronto, from the *Plain Dealer*, and the state of Ohio would be informed.

Now to the point. The city editor did not ask me how we knew. He made no query as to the means by which I had gotten the information. His assumption was, "If you fellows say it's so, it's so."

I felt that the hectic experience of that night alone had proven the golden value of integrity and it was on this foundation block that I was more than ever determined to build my business.

3

New York at Last!

ONE of my ardent ambitions was to have an office in New York. It was not simply the lure of the big city, but the obvious future of the public relations field that attracted me. New York was the financial and communications hub of the country. Growing numbers of corporations were establishing their headquarters in Manhattan. It was clearly destined to be the center of the public relations business.

I had no idea how to get such an office started without Eastern clients. Yet I felt a way would open up. I have found in my career that whenever I had a practical objective, kept my eye on it, and thought persistently about it, somehow in some way it has been attained. And so it was with a New York office.

One day in mid-November of 1933 in Cleveland, Tom Girdler telephoned me. He said that he had just come from a meeting of the Board of Directors of American Iron and Steel Institute in New York and that the executive secretary of the Institute, Walter S. Tower, was expecting a call from me. Then he gave me the telephone number and hung up.

With this meager information, I called Mr. Tower and he asked me to come see him in New York two days hence.

When I arrived in his office in the Empire State Building, Mr. Tower explained that the leaders of the steel industry were beset by many problems of public relations growing out of the Depression and political developments in Washington. He told me what every newspaper reader already knew—namely, that the steel executives were also having difficulties with the press. He said they were without any help in this area, and that my name had been suggested as one who might be of assistance. "Are you interested," he asked. The outcome of our meeting was that my firm was retained and, after thirty years, it still is serving the Institute.

For many years the Cleveland office remained the headquarters of our firm. However in the mid-forties the New York branch had grown so rapidly that I decided to turn over virtually all of my interest in the Cleveland firm to Don Knowlton and establish a new and entirely separate organization in New York. We called the New York company Hill and Knowlton, Inc., and the old firm was named Hill and Knowlton of Cleveland. The only connection between the two organizations was that Knowlton and I each held extremely small interests in the other's firm. The similarity of names has occasionally caused some confusion, but there has been little overlapping in business, as Cleveland operates regionally while the New York organization operates nationally and internationally.

American Iron and Steel Institute, which in 1933 was to be my new client in New York, was founded in 1908 at the instigation of Judge Elbert H. Gary, chairman of United States Steel Corporation. From 1908 to 1912, the Institute functioned side by side with the American Iron and Steel Association that had been the statistical collecting agency for the industry since its inception as American Iron Association in 1855. In 1912 the Institute absorbed the Association, taking over its records and activities. The Institute continued to function largely in the realm of collecting statistics until 1933.

In that year, the New Deal had passed the National Industrial Recovery Act. Under this act, codes were to be set up for the regulation of industries with the objective of stopping cut-throat competition and ruinous price cutting. The act suspended the antitrust laws and industries were invited to work out their own codes. Otherwise the government would do it for them. The steel industry elected to devise its own code, a tedious and laborious proceeding. The directors of American Iron and Steel Institute were made the steel code authority and given the responsibility of administering and enforcing it under the jurisdiction of the NIRA.

Over the years, the Institute has continued as the fountainhead of steel statistics. In addition it has proved of great, and steadily increasing, value to the companies in the industry as a neutral meeting ground and as coordinator of research for the industry.

Its principal purposes, as outlined in its constitution, are:

1. To promote the interests of the iron and steel industry or any part or branch thereof.
2. To collect statistics and other information concerning the industry.
3. To engage in investigations and research.
4. To provide a forum for the exchange of information and discussion of problems relating to the industry.
5. To promote the use of iron and steel.

These objectives in general represent the broad field of activities of most major trade associations. A trade association can be described as a non-profit organization of business competitors formed to deal with common problems in serving its membership, its industry, and the public. There are presently some 13,000 such associations in the United States, of which about 2,000 are national in scope and the balance regional or local.

It is inherent in the objectives and activities of trade associations that public relations is one of their most important functions. In some, it is almost the sole function. My firm for many years has served as public relations counsel to a number of large trade associations in addition to American Iron and Steel Institute.

The Institute is unusual among industry organizations in a number of ways, one being that it has both company and individual members. In 1963 the Institute had 93 company members and 2,660 individual members, the latter being persons employed by company members or individuals otherwise connected with the industry.

When I assumed my new responsibility late in November, 1933, it was stipulated that I should attend all meetings of the Institute Board of Directors. This was to be of inestimable value in the work. In public relations, policy is the first and most important consideration and policy can be made only by those with the top responsibility. If I were to be of any value to the steel industry, it was important that I have the confidence of the policy-makers and learn at firsthand what they were thinking and doing about the tough problems confronting them. And from time to time it was important for them to have an outside view on the probable public reaction to their decisions. I was present at all meetings of the Board for over twenty years.

At the first Board meeting I attended, I saw lined up around the table some of the titans of American industry of that day—most of them were rugged individualists. I looked on with fascinated attention as these men carried out the business before them. At that time there were about twenty-five members of the Board. Seeing them at meeting after meeting, I came to know most of them well. I soon became aware of who the leaders of the group were; the men who were always listened to by the others with close attention and respect. At the top of this list was E. G. Grace, president of Bethlehem Steel, who in his youth had been the protégé of Charles M. Schwab. Mr. Grace was president of the Institute. He was an intense man of commanding intellect. He spoke slowly, choosing his words carefully and deliberately, always with courteous consideration of his fellow members. He was perhaps the most persuasive man I have ever known.

Among others whose words carried great weight in the Board meetings were E. T. Weir, founder of National Steel; William J. Filbert, the brilliant financial executive of United States Steel and early associate of Judge Gary; Frank Purnell, president of The Youngstown Sheet & Tube Company; Tom Girdler; C. R. Hook of Armco; and L. E. Block of Inland Steel.

Mr. Filbert was a man of particularly strong views that he expressed with force and clarity. All the members had great affection for him and liked to put him on the receiving end of good-natured raillery. They once interrupted a serious discussion to poke hilarious fun at Mr. Filbert who had arrived at the meeting late, wearing into the board room large galoshes and carrying his umbrella along with his brief case.

Mr. Grace, who had a keen sense of humor, always took the lead—along with Tom Girdler—in these kidding matches. They particularly enjoyed awakening one of the members—the likeable president of a sizeable company—who sometimes would calmly hoist his feet on the table and drop off to sleep in the midst of a heated discussion.

E. T. Weir, the founder of National Steel, was a man of deep convictions. He had an effective manner of expression that left no one in doubt about his explicit meaning. He did not always see eye-to-eye with his fellow members and at one time took his company out of the Institute for a few years. I became very fond of Mr. Weir, partly I suppose because in those early years he had more comprehension of public relations than most. Mr. Weir and C. R. Hook of Armco, along with Mr. Grace and Mr. Girdler, always could be depended upon to speak up for any sensible public relations proposal in the days when many members of the Board were giving the new idea only tentative support.

There are many other outstanding leaders in the industry of that day who linger in my memories of an exciting period. They include the men who administered American Iron and Steel Institute over the span of three decades.

The thirties were crucial years in which, as I have indicated, the industry struggled to surmount the Depression, worked with the Federal government to carry out the NIRA Code of Fair Competition, went through the throes of unionization of most of the industry by the CIO, and faced the uncertain demands posed by the outbreak of war in Europe.

The forties saw the industry called upon to help lead the way in the speeding of the mobilization of our industrial resources for war. Fortunately, this nation's steel companies had the facilities and know-how for producing steel and products of steel in large volume. They could make a fast transition to the production of steel for tanks, guns, ships and other war materiel in huge proportions.

Under the most critical pressure, the industry expanded its annual capacity from 81,600,000 tons in 1939 to 95,500,000 tons in 1945. This was 20 million tons more than the maximum steel capacity of our combined enemies. The Institute played an important part in the magnificently organized effort by the industry and defense production programs for employees and plant communities. In the latter half of this decade the industry faced the problems of readjusting these tremendously expanded resources to peacetime operations. In the late forties, also, there began the labor leaders' pressures for big boosts in wages and benefits which were to have an impact on the inflationary spirals of the fifties.

In the fifties, the industry made great technological progress, developing and producing invaluable new kinds of steels for use in everything from small consumer items to orbiting space craft. At the same time, the steel companies were hit by a series of the most costly strikes in their history. They were frustrated in their efforts to extend wage and benefit increases that would be fair to their employees and at the same time avoid contributing to the nation's inflationary crisis through an endless wage-price spiral. In this decade, also, the industry began to face mounting pressures of competition from other basic materials, such as aluminum, plastics and glass.

Throughout these years, the Institute was fortunate in having at its helm men of the stature of Walter S. Tower, Max D. Howell, and Ben Fairless, after his retirement from U.S. Steel.

Walter Tower was lent to the Institute by Bethlehem Steel for six months to meet the crisis of the NIRA code formulation. He stayed for more than eighteen years, until his retirement in 1952. He was truly a scholar in business, having taught economic geography in two large universities. Possessing an engaging personality with a touch of professorial reserve and dignity, he never lost his delightful New England sense of humor. Whenever he interviewed anyone for a job, he invariably at some point would slyly test the applicant's sense of humor. If there was no comeback, no sign of response, that applicant's chances of getting the job dropped close to zero. Not the least of Walter Tower's many talents is his command of English, with the rare ability to speak or write with equal perfection and precision.

Walter Tower won the respect of the steel leaders and in 1940 they elected him president of the Institute. He filled this office with rare distinction until he retired. He firmly believed in the public relations function and gave it every encouragement.

Max D. Howell, formerly vice president and treasurer of United States Steel Corporation, became administrative head of the Institute when Walter Tower retired.

In 1955, upon his retirement as chairman of U.S. Steel, Ben Fairless became president of the Institute, serving in that capacity until his death on New Year's Day, 1962. During that period, he devoted much of his time and his great talent for leadership to the problems of the steel industry.

When Mr. Fairless died, two groups of his former associates and friends took action to perpetuate his memory. American Iron and Steel Institute established the Benjamin F. Fairless Memorial Medal to be available for awarding annually to a distinguished citizen in any field for service generally related to the preservation of economic freedom and human liberty. The first award of this medal was made in May, 1963 to Dwight D. Eisenhower. Also, a group of friends and admirers established at Carnegie Institute of Technology the Benjamin F. Fairless Memorial Lectures, to be delivered as a series annually by an outstanding American, beginning in November of 1963.

Max Howell succeeded Mr. Fairless as president, continuing as administrative head and serving until his retirement in the spring of 1963.

It was my good fortune to work closely with these three men over a period of many years. Each took a broad view of public relations for the industry and encouraged its development. When Max Howell came to the Institute in 1952, he quickly delved into the work and familiarized himself with its ramifications, with the result that he became a strong advocate of the effort to inform the public about the industry and its problems. In this he had the full support of Ben Fairless. One of Max Howell's most notable achievements for the steel industry was his promulgation and carrying through to completion of the magnificent steel exhibit in 1962 at the Chicago Museum of Science and Industry.

The new president, John P. Roche, is a man of broad experience in industry and public affairs, and is carrying on in the tradition of his predecessors.

Another man who served the industry well in the past and was a powerful factor in shaping and guiding steel's public relations was Edward L. Ryerson. He was chairman of Inland Steel and from May 25, 1944 to May 26, 1954 served as chairman of the public relations committee of the Institute's Board of Directors.

He was studious and clear-headed and animated by a deep desire for the steel industry to follow policies truly in the public interest. The confidence of the board members in him and their respect for him were so great that, in all the years he headed the public relations committee, I never knew of a single proposal or request of his to be turned down. On June 11, 1962, Yale University conferred on him an honorary doctorate of laws, together with a small group of other distinguished men including President John F. Kennedy.

Working with men of such caliber and breadth of vision as these has made our labors for the steel industry an unforgettably pleasant experience over the past thirty years.

When I came to American Iron and Steel Institute in 1933, public relations was in a primitive state in steel as well as in most other industries. Actually in all the steel industry there were only four public relations directors. W. T. Mossman of Jones & Laughlin was the dean, having been the first public relations man to appear in the industry, although he never used the title. John C. Long of Bethlehem Steel, Hugh Wright of Armco and John D. Ubinger of National Steel completed the earliest roster. J. Carlisle MacDonald of United States Steel appeared on the scene shortly thereafter. Of this pioneer group only Ubinger is still active at National Steel and as chairman of the Institute's Public Relations Program Committee. As the years went on, company after company appointed public relations officers.

4

The Storm Gathers

UNDER the NIRA steel code, price cutters and "chiselers" were to be run out of the market place. Most of the steel men looking down the road did not relish the idea of the "corporate state," but conditions were such that they recognized something had to be done. Steel operations had fallen below 15 per cent of capacity at the bottom in 1932. Prices had tobogganed and the outlook was grim.

In addition to all their other pressures, the steel leaders were faced with a swelling demand for unionization of the industry. The New Deal had drawn a bead on steel as the number-one target for labor organization. The industry sensed trouble in the offing.

There had not been a strike in steel since the abortive Communist-inspired one in 1919 and nobody wanted another. The industry leaders accepted the fact that individual bargaining no longer was practical in steel; that large aggregations of employees must have representation. They hoped that the "employee representation" plans that had been adopted in most steel plants would suffice. The labor movement, with the support of the New Deal, would brook none of this, however, and branded the employee plans as "company unions."

It seemed to me that unionization of the steelworkers was inevitable unless the industry could devise some dramatic move to meet the problem. I had the idea of a confederation of the company employee representation plans. At least the officers of such a confederation would have been authentic steelworkers steeped in the steel tradition. This might be preferable, I thought, to a union created by outside professional agitators and organizers.

I put the idea before a small group of steel executives meeting in Mr. Grace's office in New York between Christmas and New Year's in 1933. It was discussed at length and given serious consideration but nothing came of it, partly because the tide of events was moving too rapidly and inexorably toward unionization. The passage of the Wagner Act in 1935 put great monopoly power over the economy into the hands of big unions and placed the Federal government squarely behind the unionization of the big industries. The steel industry and many others vigorously protested this bill before a congressional committee but to no avail.

When the NIRA was knocked out by the Supreme Court in the "sick chicken" case in 1935, the Institute directors no longer had a code to administer. But the Institute had grown greatly in stature and in importance to the companies. Many problems of an industrywide nature were facing them and the Institute would be of increasing usefulness to the industry.

From the beginning of my work at the Institute, it was evident that there was to be no letup on the labor front. The pot began to boil when late in 1935 John L. Lewis formed his CIO and announced his intention to organize the steel industry. As the situation grew more tense, the steel leaders in 1936 resolved to make a statement putting their position on record before their employees and the public. It was decided to run this statement in the form of a full-page newspaper advertisement in order to insure its printing exactly as written all over the country.

Our small public relations group was given the assignment of writing the statement. After our text had been completed, it was turned over to the lawyers for review. They came up with a version of their own and it was approved by the executives.

Some of us were quite unhappy about this, not because of any pride of authorship, but because we felt our statement would serve the industry better. We believed the industry should say that its employees were free to choose whether they would or would not join a union but that no union should be permitted to use coercion and violence. And our version revolved on this point. The mood of the times made it clear, in our view, that the industry would gain stronger support from the public and its employees by taking this position.

I had both versions of the statement set in type and, on a very confidential basis, I showed them to a few top newspaper editors whose views on matters of public opinion were worthy of respect. One of these was the late Geoffrey Parsons, then chief of the editorial page of the *New York Herald Tribune*. Mr. Parsons read each of the ads carefully without any inkling of the source of either. He expressed unqualified preference for the one written by the public relations people.

I wrote a letter to Mr. Grace urging reconsideration of the statement before it appeared in the newspapers. Mr. Grace had an open mind and he responded by inviting Walter Tower and me to lunch at a Wall Street club to discuss the matter. On arrival I was startled to find two other guests—former Governor Nathan Miller and Hoyt A. Moore of the

Cravath firm, both eminent lawyers. I fully expected them to give me a hard time. At first I think they were inclined to do so, probably because, like most lawyers of that day, they regarded public relations people as interlopers in the corporate arena.

However, there was full discussion of the problem. The result was that, with the aid of Walter Tower, a number of language modifications were evolved. Most importantly, it was agreed that the industry, in its public statement, should avow its acceptance of the principles of collective bargaining. At the same time, it was made clear that the industry felt this was now in effect with the employee representation plans and that the disrupting interference of outside organizers was not welcome. The actual text inserted on these points read:

> The Steel Industry believes in the principle of collective bargaining, and it is in effect throughout the industry.
>
> The overwhelming majority of the employees in the Steel Industry recently participated in annual elections under their own representation plans and elected their representatives for collective bargaining. The elections were conducted by the employees themselves by secret ballot. One of the purposes of the announced campaign is to overthrow those plans and the representatives so elected.

The ad as finally run made no reference to the point we had urged; that there be a declaration of the principle that employees were "free to choose to join or not to join a union." But failure of the industry to make such a declaration was not of long-lasting significance. Time and mounting political pressures were soon to bring a complete turnabout in management's attitudes toward collective bargaining.

As legal counsel to the Institute, Mr. Moore cooperated with me freely many times after this meeting and we formed a friendship of many years' standing. He never once mentioned the fact that I had complained about the lawyer-prepared statement. In his youth he had been an English instructor and he never lost his passion for perfection of syntax and punctuation. He would spend hours on end constructing and reconstructing sentences and paragraphs and working over commas and semicolons, sometimes to the despair of an impatient and less purist-minded client.

The Institute had no further occasion to use newspaper advertising for more than a decade. By this time there was no longer any question about whether the advertising copy should be prepared by lawyers or public relations people. The latter got the assignment as a matter of course. This was a change of vast significance for public relations that came about gradually over the years in steel and in many other industries. It came as the people engaged in the new work of public relations were able to demonstrate their competence, judgment and trustworthiness. It was in no sense a reflection on lawyers, but simply an allocation of certain tasks to people with special skill and training for them.

In May of 1937, having signed a union contract with the United States Steel Corporation, John Lewis called an "organizing" strike against a number of the so-called "independent" steel companies.

It was obvious that this was to be a tough struggle because Communist agitators were everywhere in evidence around the steel plants. At the general meeting of American Iron and Steel Institute in May, 1937, when the strike was imminent, I talked seriously with Tom Girdler and Charlie White of Republic Steel about plans for the strike. They both agreed with me that everything possible should be done to avoid any outbreak of violence. After the strike started, Republic Steel inaugurated the first "air lift" in history. At the plant in Warren, Ohio, a large group of employees refused to walk off the job and stayed in the plant. Pickets—most of whom were outsiders imported for the job—barred delivery of food to them. Girdler organized a fleet of small aircraft and sent food to the embattled men. It was dropped to the ground in the plant as the planes flew over—at that time a dramatic spectacle.

Tom Girdler became the unofficial spokesman for the "Little Steel" companies that were struck and, as such, he was the target of labor and New Deal attacks. The most vicious of these centered about the Memorial Day riot at the Republic Chicago plant. A marching, shouting, club-swinging mob of some two thousand persons had been organized in the vicinity of the plant by Communist agitators. According to reliable reports, only a small number of Republic employees were in the crowd. About one thousand four hundred employees were inside the plant grounds. Since it was a holiday, only some four hundred of these were on duty, for maintenance, but all were under siege by the mob and had to stay for their own safety.

The rioters, inflamed and urged on by their organizers, violently attacked a line of Chicago city police stationed well outside the plant. The police, in self-defense, started firing and killed three of the rioters. Seven others died in hospitals later. Of the ten dead, only one was a Republic employee. Of sixty-seven arrested, only fourteen were Republic employees. Twenty-eight policemen were injured.

In no time, the Illinois State Committee of the Communist Party was showering Chicago with handbills shouting that "Old Czarist Russia had its bloody Sunday but it did not save the Czar! . . . Memorial Day, 1937, becomes for us a Memorial Day for the working class heroes who died for democracy in Chicago." The Communists demanded the "indictment" of Girdler "for his conspiracy to violate the Wagner Labor Relations Law by force and violence"; and urged that "all trade union workers and liberal organizations unite and give full support to the CIO."

The union in turn took up the cry, calling Tom Girdler a "murderer," and one of President Roosevelt's cabinet members, Harold Ickes, sarcastically referred to Girdler as the "hero of the Memorial Day massacre in Chicago." Girdler had been nowhere near Chicago. Apparently his "crime" was his insistence that the 23,000 Republic employees who wanted to stay on their jobs in various plant cities be permitted to do so.

Overnight Girdler became a controversial figure around the country. Many persons then and since have felt that his opposition to the CIO drive was a hopeless cause, that he was up against a massive political juggernaut bent on serving the union leaders, and that he should have bowed to the inevitable. But, right or wrong, that was not the way of Tom Girdler.

Actually, neither he nor any of his fellow steel leaders were against fair wages and good working conditions for labor. They were *for* these things. In his autobiographical book, *Boot Straps*, published in 1943, Girdler wrote:

> I am not against unions. I never have been against unions ... I don't question the right of any man to stop work or change his employment when it suits him but for the life of me I cannot be made to believe such a right can be expanded justly into a right to interfere wholesale with the rights of other Americans. I do not wish workers to give up any proper power they now possess to improve their lot. I have come to believe that unions are necessary but I cannot make myself believe that unions have any right whatsoever to accomplish their will by violence.

The steel leaders did believe and did say that if great labor union monopolies were to be formed, these powerful monopolies would be in a position to weaken or even strangle the whole economy. It was as much against the public interest to have unregulated labor unions, Girdler declared, as it once was to have unregulated corporations. As the years rolled on, events were to prove the correctness of these views, but the popular will was on the side of the New Deal and nothing could stop it. Yet, even to this day the issue of labor union monopoly is very much alive and unsolved, as was stated in the report of President Kennedy's Labor Management Advisory Committee on May 1, 1962.

In an addendum to that report, some of the members of the Committee asserted that the public should be protected by law from the monopoly power of the labor unions just as the antitrust laws had been applied to business. Joseph L. Block, chairman of Inland Steel Company, declared that "the occurrence of national emergency disputes" was "due in large part to the monopoly power which enables a union (or a combination of unions) to call a strike that brings to a halt all, or the preponderance of, the production in a vital industry." He suggested that "this power . . . be curbed by law, just as Congress has protected the public by enacting the antitrust laws to prevent business from having monopolistic powers."

He said further that "the enactment of such legislation would go a long way toward eliminating the need for governmental intervention in collective bargaining, though the public interest would still need protection in special situations such as defense operations and vital links in our transportation facilities."

The day was to come, too, when articulate civic leaders and publications would increasingly be calling attention to the problem. For example, Louis B. Seltzer, the highly respected editor of the *Cleveland Press and News*, would declare in February of 1963:

> It is my own judgment that labor is behaving excessively in America today just as business, the banks, the stock market, the utilities, the railroads did in their time in the past.
>
> In each of these other instances the United States Government, in the interest of all the people, was required to step in and, by enactment of legislation, control these excesses and eliminate the abuses. The same situation now prevails with labor.

The magazine *Time* in its issue of March 1, 1963, had this to say:

> ...for an abundance of reasons—aging leadership, corruption and inability to keep pace with technological progress, above all the fact that it has often subordinated public welfare to private gain—labor is doing what it can least afford. It is losing public support to a critical degree.
>
> On that single fact, there is remarkable agreement...It was put another way by Labor Pundit Paul Jacobs, a longtime union representative, who is now at the University of California's Institute of Industrial Relations. Said Jacobs: "The community at large became disenchanted with Big Labor right after the war. It was disenchanted at the time of the McClellan hearings. And it is disenchanted now. But what is new is that the liberal and social-welfare groups are also disenchanted."

Statements such as these echo the warnings and forecasts iterated and reiterated many times in the hectic days of the thirties.

5

The "Bombshell" that Fizzled

AFTER the "Little Steel" strike in 1937, there were two congressional investigations concerning it. One of these hearings was before the Senate Post Office Committee that was investigating the stoppage of the mails during the strike by the CIO. It was presided over by the late Senator Josiah Bailey of South Carolina. Senator Allen J. Ellender of Louisiana was an active participant. This hearing was fair. Tom Girdler was given full opportunity to state his case. This he did well both in a statement to the Committee and in his answers to questions from the members of the Committee.

I had worked on the opening statement with Thomas F. Patton, young general counsel, and Joseph Voss, industrial relations vice president, and others, until five o'clock in the morning. Copies of it were ready for the ample press contingent when the hearings started and the papers next day gave the hearing full and favorable coverage. Next morning I and other members of the Girdler entourage were scheduled to fly back to Cleveland for a meeting. All in all the hearing had gone well, but it was to have some side effects that caused a number of sleepless nights for me.

It had so happened that a friendly and well-meaning Senator had advised Mr. Girdler to retain a Washington public relations counsel and he had done so a few days before. This appeared to be a good move, but I was alarmed when the new Washington counsel suggested a press conference for Mr. Girdler on the day following the hearing. Because of the excellent press, it seemed obvious to all of us that the best thing for Mr. Girdler to do was to rest on his laurels for the moment. Thereupon the new Washington counsel proposed a strictly off-the-record press luncheon in Mr. Girdler's suite and it was agreed that this be done. Reassured that no statements would be made to the press, all of us in the Republic group except Mr. Girdler flew off to Cleveland.

That afternoon about four o'clock my office in Cleveland got word of an alarming news dispatch from Washington. The story concerned a purported statement by Mr. Girdler in which he had spoken most unkindly of some of the steel company heads who did not see eye-to-eye with him on his labor union views. "My God," I groaned, "the fat is in the fire."

I called Mr. Girdler in Washington to ask whether he actually had given such a statement. He had checked out of the hotel and was on his way to Cleveland. Then I called the writer of the story, but he had gone off to the woods somewhere for the weekend. Calls to other newsmen who had attended the luncheon brought the unanimous assurance that Mr. Girdler had given out no statement whatever in keeping with the "off-the-record" character of the luncheon. Although I could not reach Mr. Girdler to get a flat repudiation of the story, I nevertheless called the wire service that had it and told the managing editor of the circumstances. He promised to investigate the matter immediately and promised he would send out a "kill" to newspapers if he could reach the writer of the story and get his confirmation that no quotes had been authorized. Apparently he could not find the writer either, because the story appeared under big headlines in the morning papers.

When I saw Mr. Girdler next morning he was shocked and angry that such a story had been printed. Had I been able to get him the evening before, he of course would have repudiated it. Now a denial would get nowhere. As I expected, the incident created a stir in steel circles. Some members of the Steel Institute Board of Directors, unaware of the facts, thought I was responsible for the offending news story. Finally a special meeting of the executive committee of the Board was called to consider the matter of my continued retention by the Institute. The outcome of that session was a unanimous vote of confidence for me.

The other congressional hearing growing out of the strike was presided over by Senator Robert M. LaFollette and it was totally unfair. One evening in a Washington night club during the hearing, I met various members of the LaFollette committee staff, male and female, who were celebrating. They were exceedingly jovial and invited me to join their table. One of the staff members was a portly young man named Edward F. Prichard, Jr. He had been a secretary to a Supreme Court Justice and was rated in New Deal circles as a clever leftist intellectual with a brilliant future.

On this evening Prichard was expansive and happy. "We're doing a great job in the committee for the CIO," he boasted to me. "It will do the organizing trick for them." Then, growing confidential, he told me the staff was preparing to drop a bombshell in the lap of my firm at the committee hearings in a day or two.

"It's the first time a public relations firm ever has been put on the grill in a congressional hearing," he said. "And we all are wondering what the result will be. Some of the boys think it will put you out of business. I hope not, but we're going to keep you guessing about our bombshell."

I thanked him for the information and left. The "bombshell" proved to be a memorandum taken from our files and written by one of our staff members to a client. It contained a wholly innocent but unfortunately phrased sentence that could be twisted into meaning that the client was advised to use the "pressure" of advertising in connection with a hostile newspaper.

Any such advice would have violated the principles and practices of our firm. But to Senator LaFollette, the memorandum was a juicy morsel and he proceeded to make the most of it. He read the brief document into the record with his unfavorable interpretation just before adjournment of the afternoon session and handed out mimeograph copies to the press. We were given no chance at all to clarify the memorandum or to refute his interpretation of it. So, on the basis of a single casual sentence in an isolated memorandum that admittedly did not reflect the policy of our firm, we were to be destroyed.

But the effort failed because neither this so-called "bombshell" nor later grilling of me and my partner, Don Knowlton, put us out of business. Ten years later, in an article in *Collier's* magazine, of February 8, 1947, LaFollette acknowledged the unfairness of his hearings and declared that his staff in the investigation had been dominated by Communist sympathizers.

He wrote: "I know from first-hand experience that Communist sympathizers have infiltrated into committee staffs on Capitol Hill in Washington. A few years ago, when I was chairman of the Senate Civil Liberties Committee, I was forced to take measures in an effort to stamp out influences within my own committee staff."

How he could have failed to be aware of this from the

outset was beyond my understanding. As might have been expected under such auspices, the hearings were handled much like a Soviet purge trial, with no attempt at fairness or even decency. And yet these hearings are now on the record, form the basis of study by researchers to this day, and nourish an entirely erroneous picture of labor-management relations and company attitudes of the period.

Prichard, who had so gleefully engineered the blow at my firm, later returned to his home state of Kentucky to enter politics. In time, he landed in the penitentiary on conviction for election frauds.

The "Little Steel" strike had ended without victory for the new Lewis union. The companies did not sign a contract, and Tom Girdler declared privately he would never deal with the union unless ordered to by the Supreme Court. This was something of a retreat from a statement he had made a year or two earlier before a group in New York. Then he said, speaking extemporaneously, that "rather than do business with John Lewis and Bill Green," he would go back to his farm in Ohio and raise apples. This statement was widely quoted in the press and came back to plague him for years. But it served one useful purpose in making him much more cautious about giving out off-the-cuff public statements.

Actually, on April 12, 1937, the Supreme Court in the case of National Labor Relations Board vs. Jones & Laughlin Steel Corporation upheld the constitutionality of the National Labor Relations Act. However, that in itself did not obligate the companies to bargain with the Steelworkers Union, because the union had not been certified as a bargaining agency. The union made no gains in the 1937 organizing strike, but in 1939 it started a vigorous campaign of organization.

By late summer of 1942, a number of companies, including Republic Steel, had signed collective bargaining agreements with the union. The Republic contract was concluded in Pittsburgh on August 11. It was signed by the company's industrial relations director, J. A. Voss, and a number of union officials, headed by CIO president Philip Murray.

Girdler afterwards stated that, as law-abiding citizens, he and his associates had acceded promptly when the Supreme Court ruled that labor union agreements must be written contracts. They intended to do their best, he said, to make the new relationship work to the advantage of the employees and the company; and he noted that union officials had commented favorably on the progress. "But," he added typically, "this does not mean that my opinions have changed."

All of these companies that signed agreements, in fact, set out assiduously to make the new relationship work to the best advantage of all parties. Actually, in the intervals between strikes—in the day-to-day working out of problems and grievances—the United Steelworkers Union and the steel companies have worked together with a surprising degree of mutual goodwill and cooperation.

After one of the Washington hearings, I went to the Seignory Club in Canada for a short vacation. There at the same time was my good friend, the handsome and able young general counsel for Republic Steel, Tom Patton. We rode horseback and played golf together. One day on the golf course, he said he had received a tempting offer to join a big law firm and was trying to make up his mind. "Do you think it would be better for me to stay with the company or go to the law firm?" he asked.

It was a difficult question to answer, because obviously with his ability he would make his mark anywhere, but my own feeling was, I told him, that the law firm would give him a wider field of activity than being "tied to one company." But, fortunately for him, he didn't take my counsel. Today Tom Patton is one of America's outstanding industrial leaders—president of Republic Steel Corporation and chairman of American Iron and Steel Institute, and a director of American Telephone & Telegraph Co.

One of the things to be done for American Iron and Steel Institute at the beginning of my work there was to get it established as a recognized source of trustworthy information about the steel industry. The purpose was to capitalize upon its expanded statistical program. As a step toward this end, I suggested a publication and this was started in mid-1934.

It was called *Steel Facts*. The Institute directors liked it but some advised against any commitment to put out the publication on a regular basis. They feared we would soon run out of good material. My own opinion was that an industry so basic as steel would provide an endless flow of material for *Steel Facts*, and this has proven to be true. The first issue had a distribution of 5,000 and today it is read by around 200,000 people. In all, 173 issues have appeared and *Steel Facts* has become a widely accepted and broadly quoted source of steel industry information. For any important enterprise or industry, a well-edited publication is a valuable public relations tool. My firm has recommended and developed many such publications and all have been considered successful. These publications provide one straightforward way of taking an industry's story directly to the public.

Immediately after the war, I proposed a series of innovations in the Institute's public relations. One was a new magazine called *Steelways*. It occurred to me that, whereas *Steel Facts* devoted itself largely to dramatizing and publicizing the statistical side of the industry, a publication was needed to do these things for the human and economic side in order to bring an understanding of the steel industry and some of its many facets to more people. I developed a "dummy" for such a magazine and in doing it I bent over backwards to keep the cost low.

When I presented this "dummy" to the Institute executive committee, consisting of Messrs. Ryerson, Grace, Fairless, Weir, Girdler, and a few others, they looked it over thoughtfully. "We like the idea," was the verdict, "but this doesn't look commensurate with the importance of the steel industry. Get up something a little more impressive," they said. Accordingly, in a few months I came back with a far more handsome version and it was promptly approved. *Steelways* today is eighteen years old and by professional tests has the highest readership of any industry magazine in the country.

In the thirties and onward, major public relations problems were constantly arising for steel, in not all of which the Institute participated. One of these in 1938 was the famous TNEC investigation in Congress headed by Senator Joseph C. O'Mahoney. TNEC stood for Temporary National Economic Committee. Its avowed purpose was to aid the economy, but many regarded it as a thinly veiled attack upon industry, not only steel, but various others.

As the big guns of the probers were trained on the United States Steel Corporation, that company was fully prepared when its time came to appear. Its presentation was a masterwork of comprehensive and illuminating facts about the vast scope of the company's operations from mine to mill. When this presentation was completed, it had supplied sweepingly convincing answers to the critics of steel and for a brief time they were quiet. The man who had directed this massive work was Irving S. Olds of the White & Case law firm, legal counsel for U.S. Steel and later its chairman. His chief assistant in marshaling the facts was a young lawyer from his firm. After the TNEC investigation, I saw the young lawyer on many occasions, usually at hearings or meetings in Washington. He attracted my notice because when he spoke, it was to the point, carefully thought out, and wholly devoid of flamboyance of manner. Little did anyone know that this young lawyer, whose name was Roger M. Blough, was headed for the chairmanship of the world's largest steel company—U.S. Steel.

The steel industry and the whole economy really got under way to full recovery from the Great Depression in 1939. Then the revival that the New Deal could not induce was fanned into being by World War II. The steel industry swung into high gear, a situation that was to last for many years. Concentration was centered upon war production and all output for this purpose had top priority over everything else. One of our big public relations jobs at the Institute was to participate in the steel scrap collection drive under the general direction of Robert W. Wolcott, then president of Lukens Steel Co. and chairman of the Institute Scrap Committee.

This was one of the first important public service jobs undertaken by the nation's advertising agencies through the newly formed Advertising Council. The scrap-ad campaign plan was developed by Leo Burnett and put into action by McCann-Erickson. Publicity was one part of the job and this was our responsibility. To help in this effort I called on two good friends, James P. Selvage and Morris Lee, who had recently started their firm, Selvage & Lee. Since the war, the Advertising Council has continued year by year to carry on an extraordinarily effective public service in support of many worthy causes. Since 1957 it has been my privilege to serve on its Board of Directors.

After World War II, the steel industry was under intense pressure from President Truman's group of Fair Deal economists to expand greatly steel's producing capacity. The issue had grown so warm that a Senate committee called leading company heads to appear at a hearing on the subject. There was a general feeling in the industry that the Washington pressure was unjustified and was taking on the form of political harassment.

A meeting of the twelve steel leaders who had been subpoenaed to testify was held at the Institute in New York on the day before they were to be in Washington. On the same day a meeting of the Institute's public relations committee was called. We were supposed to help devise some kind of strategy that would protect the industry from senatorial castigation. The prospect looked pretty grim when someone had a bright idea. It was to ascertain from the assembled steel officials if any expansion was being planned by their companies and if so how much

The company heads fell in with our idea and each wrote the figure for his company on a piece of paper. When these were added, the total came to $500,000,000. The huge amount took everyone by surprise and a dramatic change in attitude came over the group. Clearly here was the strategy ready made. Just tell the Senate committee the facts and let them speak for themselves. This is exactly what was done by the steel executives when they appeared before the Senate committee the next day. The result was that the wind was taken out of the sails of the New Deal critics on the expansion issue. But, of course, the plans for increased capacity were no mere stunt concocted for the Senate committee. In the decade to follow, steel capacity was expanded so rapidly that later the question was raised whether the industry had overexpanded.

As public relations activities for the Institute increased with the passing of time, an enlarged staff was necessary and the Institute asked my firm to provide it. This freed the administrators of the organization of the burden of selecting and supervising people in the specialized work of public relations. Other large clients from time to time have asked us to assume a similar responsibility.

In addition to steel, as the years went on, other large clients began to appear. One of these was the Shipbuilders Council of America. During the war the shipbuilders of our country performed miracles in the production of ships to bridge two oceans. They contributed mightily to America's victory. Shipbuilding ballooned into an enormous industry overnight and many problems in public relations developed. The most amazing job in turning out ships with speed and competence was that of Bethlehem Steel's shipbuilding division. E. G. Grace had put the management responsibility of this division upon the broad shoulders of an able young man who knew shipbuilding inside and out. He did so well that Mr. Grace brought him into the steel side and today, the one-time shipbuilder, now steel man, Arthur B. Homer is chairman and chief executive officer of the Bethlehem Steel Corporation.

My work for the steel industry always has been of absorbing interest. The most exciting, as well as exhausting, days and nights have been during periods of labor stress. Since the Institute does not engage in labor negotiations, these matters have been handled by the companies. Our firm has been retained by these companies because of the availability of a trained staff to work on the public relations aspects of the problem.

My firm has lived through the thick of all troubles in steel for three decades. The most extraordinary of all these controversies was the strike of 1952. It contained all the elements of melodrama that could possibly be imagined. The cast of characters included the President of the United States, the steel industry, the steel union, the Supreme Court, Congress and many others. In a large sense, it was a public relations battle on a broad front and, for this reason, I am recalling some of the incidents attending it.

6

The Mills Are Seized!

AT 10:29 P.M. on April 8, 1952 some thirty grim-faced steel executives were dispersed in adjoining rooms on the seventeenth floor of the Roosevelt Hotel in New York City. After weeks of futile negotiation with the steelworkers union, a strike had been called for midnight. But meanwhile the word was flashed that at 10:30 P.M. the President of the United States would speak to the nation over all radio and TV networks. It was announced that he would discuss the steel labor dispute.

The group at the Roosevelt had heard disquieting rumors and they were tensely bracing themselves for a severe tongue-lashing by the man who apparently took delight in the description of himself as "Give-em hell Harry." Exactly at 10:30 President Truman came on the air and began a bitter attack upon the steel industry. This in itself was not surprising because a steel union official just a few weeks before had told a cheering group of workers:

> We are certainly pleased in the role Harry Truman is playing in behalf of the steelworkers union in the wage

dispute since labor did so well by Mr. Truman in the polls in 1948.

What did stun the steel men was the sensational and historic announcement made by the President in the following passage:

> It is perfectly clear that the emergency provisions of the Taft-Hartley Act do not meet the needs of the present situation. The Wage Board recommendations are less than the Union thought they ought to have . . . The fact of the matter is that the settlement proposed by the Board is fair to both parties and to the public interest. And what is more, I think the steel companies know it.
>
> The plain fact of the matter is that the steel companies are recklessly forcing a shutdown of the steel mills.
>
> At midnight the government will take over the steel plants.

A deep hush fell over the group. They had expected a blow from the White House, but not this. With the mills seized, the strike was called off and operations were continuing. But who was to run the mills? The answer to that question could wait until morning. There was more immediate work to be done that night. As the President was speaking, the public relations people present, like everyone else, were in a momentary state of shock. But this was quickly over and a prompt decision was made to recommend a reply to the President on the following evening by a leading steel company spokesman.

First it was necessary to determine whether the networks would grant time. There was only one way to find out and that was to ask them. Calls were placed to the heads of all networks and the question put to them. They would give no answer that night but promised to have representatives in the

Hill and Knowlton office at nine o'clock the next morning. This looked promising and we then turned to the next problem; that of finding the right spokesman. A name occurred to several of us simultaneously. It was Clarence Randall, the brilliant, articulate, and rapier-tongued president of Inland Steel. The suggestion was passed on to Ben Fairless, then president of U.S. Steel, who liked the idea, and he arranged to have breakfast with Randall the next morning to try to get his consent.

The next day a number of steelmen were due in Washington for meetings and I had to go with them. When I left, the networks representatives were in my office working out details for the broadcast that night over all the outlets that had used Truman. Randall had consented to do the job and we offered to place writers at his disposal to assist in preparing the text. But being lawyer-trained and a skilled writer himself, he had no need for the help. His only problem was a broken inlay that had to be fixed before he could speak comfortably. A dentist was found to patch this up and all was ready for the steel industry's reply to the President of the United States. When Randall came on the air, what he said to the American people was stirring, strong and straight from the shoulder. He said in part:

> I have a deep sense of responsibility as I face this vast audience of the air. I am here to make answer on behalf of the steel industry to charges flung over these microphones last night by the man who then stood where I stand now. I am a plain citizen. He was the President of the United States. Happily we still live in a country where a private citizen may look the President in the eye and tell him that he was wrong, but actually it is not the President of the United States to whom I make answer. It is Harry S. Truman, the man, who last night so far transgressed his oath of office, so far abused the power which is temporarily his, that

he must now stand and take it. I shall not let my deep respect for the office which he holds stop me from denouncing his shocking distortions of fact. Nor shall I permit the honor of his title to blind the American people from the enormity of what he has done.

He has seized the steel plants of the nation, the private property of one million people, most of whom now hear the sound of my voice. This he has done without the slightest shadow of legal right. No law passed by the Congress gave him the power. He knows this, and speaks of general authority conferred upon him by the Constitution. But I say, my friends, that the Constitution was adopted by our forefathers to prevent tyranny, not to create it. When he asked the Congress for power to seize private property they said no. They gave him instead the Taft-Hartley Act which he now spurns, and the power which they denied him he now has seized.

The seizure of the mills, in itself historic, touched off a series of other historical events reaching into Congress and the Supreme Court. Public relations played an important role in the drama that followed. It was decided to follow up Mr. Randall's broadcast with a newspaper ad throughout the country. Although my firm does no general advertising, special situations began to arise in the late forties that made it advisable for us to have publisher recognition for the placement of ads of an emergency institutional nature during large public relations campaigns. Clients had requested this in a number of instances because it made possible quicker handling of emergency problems.

In any event, we were charged with running an advertising program during the period of mill seizure. The first ad was to be on the significance of the seizure to the people of America. I wrote the first draft over one weekend, talked over the copy with Edward Ryerson, Ben Fairless, Irving

Olds, chairman of U.S. Steel, and Carlisle MacDonald, assistant to Mr. Olds and then chairman of the Institute Public Relations Advisory Committee. Mr. Olds, a lawyer who had a fine sense of the meaning of words, went over the copy with painstaking care, making helpful suggestions. Since this was to be a statement to the people of America, I suggested a closing paragraph inviting readers to write to their congressmen and senators. The ad bore the headline, "A Threat to American Freedom." In part it said:

> Every man and woman who works, every citizen in America, has a stake in the great issues growing out of the seizure of the steel mills.
>
> If the President has the right to seize private property to enforce union demands, as has been done in steel, then both the right of property and the continuation of collective bargaining are in serious danger.
>
> Even the independence of unions, themselves, will be in jeopardy.
>
> In looking to the Administration to enforce its demands, the union confesses lack of faith in true collective bargaining. It trades political support for Government favors.
>
> How has the Administration sought to pay its debts to the union?
>
> This fight does not concern the steel companies alone. It is the fight of every American citizen.
>
> If you are opposed to the illegal seizure of property by Government to enforce labor union demands, or for any other purpose, your only recourse is in Congress.
>
> It is your privilege as an American citizen to express your views to your Congressman and Senators.

This ad was run in some four hundred newspapers. It had instant and wide response. Although we had not asked readers to write to the steel companies group sponsoring the ad, we began receiving an avalanche of mail, most of which contained copies of letters being sent to congressmen and senators. This mail came from every state in the union and in all we received some eighteen thousand such letters. No doubt other people wrote to their representatives in Congress without thinking to send us a copy, but I had no way of guessing how many.

One morning at an early hour, I read a hard-hitting editorial favorable to our side in the *New York Mirror*. It occurred to me that a reprint of this editorial would make an excellent ad for newspapers around the country. I got the consent of Glenn Neville, executive editor of the *Mirror*, and then put it up to Edward Ryerson and Ben Fairless. Both approved and the ad appeared in papers throughout the country the next morning. On April 19, *Editor & Publisher* had a story under the heading "Steel Industry Ads Handled Like Spot News." It said in part:

> Hill and Knowlton, Inc., a public relations agency that handles institutional advertising for the steel industry, is believed to have set new records this week by treating advertising as if it were news.
>
> At 11:30 A.M. Monday, H & K received approval from steel company executives on the draft of a full-page newspaper advertisement setting forth the position of the Steel Companies in the Wage Case on the government seizure of the industry. In less than 12 hours the ad was on the street in major cities throughout the U.S. It appeared in 74 Tuesday morning and evening newspapers in 26 cities.
>
> A second ad, approved in typescript at 6:30 P.M. Tuesday, appeared in print in 72 Wednesday afternoon and Thursday morning newspapers in 27 cities ranging from Boston to San Francisco and as far south as Birmingham, Ala.
>
> According to John W. Hill, president of Hill and Knowlton, stringent effort by both his staff and the newspapers

accounted for this extraordinary performance. In both cases the agency's personnel in New York, Cleveland, Washington, Pittsburgh and Chicago were on the telephone within 15 minutes after the ads were approved, reserving space in the newspapers in their cities. From New York telephone, telegraph and air mail were used to hold space in other cities. Without a single exception the newspapers agreed to reserve pages in view of the spot news aspects of the copy. *The Wall Street Journal* in New York telephoned the copy to its San Francisco office and gave instructions on typography. The San Francisco office, in turn, got in touch with the five other newspapers in the area. Then they set the type, made the matrices, and had them ready when messenger boys called for them.

The dispute had begun with the union in November, 1951 when the union served notice that it must have a new contract by December 31. The Korean War was on and there was a defense mobilization board. This board had suggested a Wage Stabilization Board that was set up by the President with Nathan Feinsinger as chairman.

On December 21, 1951, the steel companies formally put forward their position that both parties should agree to hold the line against inflation. A statement issued by Benjamin F. Fairless, president of U.S. Steel, said in part:

> Everyone should recognize that inflation is the major enemy of this country at this moment... The nation cannot now afford another general round of substantial wage increases and the higher prices which must inevitably result therefrom... Any such increase in our wages would smash into bits the Government's existing wage stabilization formula... That is why I believe there should be no wage or price increase at this time.

This proposal would have required a sacrifice on the part of the companies of a price increase to which they then were clearly entitled under the Capehart Amendment to the Defense Production Act of 1950. Congress enacted the Capehart Amendment to provide for price increases to compensate for increases in the cost of production that took place between the outbreak of the Korean War and July 26, 1951. Price control and stabilization officials later conceded that under this amendment steel companies were entitled to a price increase of almost $3 a ton, even before the union ever submitted a demand for a wage increase. Therefore, when the steel companies submitted a "hold-the-line" proposal, they were volunteering to give up a price increase to which they were entitled as a matter of law, in the hope of preventing a new inflationary spiral in prices and living costs.

The union's position on holding the line already had been well-reflected in a statement by Joseph P. Malony, the union's regional director at Buffalo, who said: "We're not going to pierce the Wage Stabilization Board formula, we're not going to bend it—we're going to break it."

On December 22 the President referred the matter to the Wage Stabilization Board, with the general understanding that its findings would not be binding on either side.

The union called off the strike scheduled to take place upon expiration of its contracts at midnight, December 31, 1951, following an assurance by the President to Mr. Murray that the Taft-Hartley Act would not be invoked.

After extended hearings, the WSB came up with recommendations calling for an increase in direct employment costs of nearly 30 cents an hour. This was scored by the industry members of the board as excessive and inflationary. The companies rejected the WSB proposals.

Then came one of the strangest episodes involving a President in American history. Defense Mobilizer Charles E. Wilson was charged by President Truman with settling the dispute.

Belatedly informed of the Wage Board recommendations on the day they were made public, he flew to Key West where the President was vacationing. He went to inform the President that the recommendations were inflationary, should not be adopted *in toto*, and would require a substantial price increase for the steel companies to meet even part of the recommendations.

Upon his return from Key West on Monday, March 24, Mr. Wilson was asked by the press whether the WSB action would adversely affect stabilization for the country. Mr. Wilson, thinking he had President Truman's support, answered the question bluntly: "Of course it would. If they become final, it would have a tremendous effect on the stabilization plans of the country and would lead to, in my judgment, inflation to a very serious degree."

Much disturbed by the train of events and eager as ever to avert a steel strike, six leading steel companies agreed on Friday, March 28, to meet jointly the following Monday with union representatives in an effort to reach agreement along the lines suggested by Defense Mobilizer Wilson, in conformity, he thought, with instructions from the President.

Friday afternoon, however, President Truman reversed his instructions to Mr. Wilson to settle the steel dispute. Mr. Wilson later stated his belief that this change followed a telephone call from Mr. Murray or one of his aides to the President or his staff at Key West. By Sunday, March 30, Mr. Wilson had resigned the nation's top defense mobilization job, saying, "I cannot accept public responsibility for national stabilization actions which I cannot control." The companies' understanding with Mr. Wilson, which led to the March 28 agreement to start negotiations, was out the window.

This unexpected development postponed the joint company and union meetings scheduled for March 31. Steel company officials meeting in New York with the union during the first week in April made first one, then a second wage offer to the union. The first called for a basic wage increase of 9 cents an hour plus costly benefits. The second offer was for a 12½ cent basic pay rise plus other benefits that would have cost the companies a total of 20 cents an hour.

The union rejected both propositions and insisted on obtaining the full WSB recommendations. From then on, the union treated the recommendations as a mandate to be enforced without modification of any sort. In this they were repeatedly supported by President Truman.

When seizure took place, the major companies immediately challenged in the courts the legality of the President's action.

Reaction in Congress and throughout the country was almost universally one of shock, indignation, and protest. Even the few who believed Federal seizure was the answer thought the authority for such action should come from Congress, not from the alleged inherent powers of the President.

Congress immediately went into action. Some congressmen proposed impeachment of the President. The Senate voted to withhold funds to finance the government operation of the mills. The House overwhelmingly was for an investigation of the Wage Stabilization Board.

The direct result of the various congressional investigations was action by Congress reconstituting the WSB and sharply restricting its powers.

The American system of checks and balances now began to operate. On April 29, Judge David A. Pine ruled that there was "utter and complete lack of authoritative support" for the Presidential seizure of private property and ruled that the steel facilities should be turned back to their owners.

Immediately Mr. Murray ordered a strike, even though the plants were still under government control. Not until the

U.S. Circuit Court of Appeals suspended Judge Pine's ruling pending a decision by the Supreme Court of the United States, did the union permit workers to go back to their jobs.

On May 2, both the government and the steel companies asked the Supreme Court to take the case directly, and that the court agreed to do. Justices of the Supreme Court ordered the government not to impose the WSB recommendations while the court was considering the legality of the seizure.

The period during which the Supreme Court was considering the steel-seizure issue was one of relative calm. This calm ended at noon on June 2 when the Supreme Court of the United States ruled 6 to 3 that the seizure was an unconstitutional act on the part of the President. President Truman promptly ordered the Secretary of Commerce to turn back the steel properties to the companies, thus concluding the seizure episodes.

Thirty-five minutes after the Supreme Court spoke, the steelworkers were ordered out on strike. In Congress, many voices urged the President to invoke the Taft-Hartley law, but he apparently had given his word that there would be no Taft-Hartley proceeding.

On June 10, the President went before the Congress with a request that it give him legislative power to seize and operate the mills. Instead, Congress voted by a large majority to request him to use Taft-Hartley.

As the strike went into its eighth week, the need for settlement became urgent but no settlement was in sight. The army was forced to shut down an artillery shell-making plant from lack of steel. Secretary of Defense Robert Lovett said the "stoppage" was a calamity because of the Korean War. Terrific pressures were mounting throughout the country for an end of the strike.

Finally, on July 24, President Truman called Ben Fairless

and Philip Murray into his office and said that there must be an end to the strike. He then gave the two men their orders. He told them they were to go into an adjacent room, lock the door, and stay there until a settlement had been reached. Because of the tremendous pressures upon them for a settlement and because the area of difference had narrowed, they found they could reach an understanding with reference to the final thorny issue—a modified union shop—within five minutes. Ben Fairless later told about the meeting in an article in *Life* magazine of August 4, 1952.

> We were ushered into an outer office and left alone. Within five minutes Murray had accepted our compromise and the whole thing was settled. I said, "Fine, let's go tell the President." Murray said, "Oh, no. Think of all those newspapermen out there. We've got to make this look more difficult." So we sat and talked baseball and swapped jokes. Murray, a good Catholic, told me a story about a priest at a prizefight which I have always liked and often used in speeches. The priest, an old fight fan, took along a Protestant minister who had never seen any boxing. In the first fight one of the boys crossed himself before leaving his corner. "Father, will that help him?" the Protestant asked. "It will if he can fight," said the priest.

Their conversation swung back to the strike and the steel man asked the union leader to tell him what the real basic cause of the trouble was. "Is it down in the plant?" he asked, "or is it at our level?" "Yes," the labor leader replied, "it is down in the plant. I am sure of that."

Out of this discussion came the idea of joint tours by the heads of the steel company and of the labor union to meet and talk with the workers face to face. After an hour Murray said: "All right let's go" and they broke off their talk session and announced that the strike was over.

The strike settlement called for a wage increase of 12½ cents an hour and benefits, as well as a modified union shop. A price increase was approved by the government to cover a small part of the greater employment costs.

The announcement of the proposed joint tours was made at a large press conference at the Mayflower Hotel. Phil Murray did not live to carry out his part. He died in California some time later. But his successor, David McDonald, went though with it and the famous Fairless-McDonald meetings with workers were held in the company's plants throughout the country. They were widely acclaimed as a forward step in employee relations in the steel industry.

In this way, the long, drawn-out 1952 steel controversy was finally settled. Steelworkers lost more than 400 million dollars in wages, hundreds of thousands of workers in other lines were laid off, and more fuel was poured on the fires of inflation.

From the beginning, the steel companies were deeply conscious of their obligation to exert every possible effort to help stop the inflation spiral. In that spirit they had proposed that both parties agree to "hold the line" on wages and prices, even though such a policy involved a sacrifice by the companies of the price increase to which they were already entitled under the Capehart Amendment of 1951. However, hopes of "holding the line" waned with the startling Wage Stabilization Board recommendations. They disappeared altogether when President Truman promptly sided with the union and pronounced the all-time record wage increase proposed by the WSB as "fair and reasonable." Thus the public once again was forced to pay the inflation toll levied by the union-government alliance.

All through virtually every scene in this long and tense melodrama, public relations played an active role. Steel industry public relations men and counsel were always close at hand during the bargaining sessions.

The industry's public relations men also worked around the clock to supply requests for information from the press, radio, and TV about all of these administrative, legislative, and judicial procedures and the companies' viewpoints with regard to them. In fact, "around the clock" was a good description of the working schedules for steel industry public relations men from November, 1951 until July 24, 1952.

This was probably one of the largest public relations activities of our time. Each of the major steel companies loaned one or more of its public relations executives to Hill and Knowlton to assist in meeting this enormous work load. In addition, my firm hired numerous additional specialists for the duration of the strike.

Operating from our headquarters in the Empire State Building, this enlarged staff engaged in virtually all kinds of public relations activity and employed every known communications tool. Material presented before congressional committees was reprinted and widely distributed; television talks were reprinted and widely distributed; motion pictures; booklets; direct presentations to editors and writers; innumerable press conferences; the creation of a news network that could make instantaneous release of the steel companies' announcements in all the major cities of the United States—these were only a few of the far-reaching activities that were employed to inform the public of the facts.

There have been other strikes in steel since 1952, but none has equaled that one in drama, excitement, and national interest. The most recent strike, in 1959, lasted for 116 days. It was bitter and costly but out of it came the realization on the part of both sides that some formula must be found to avert such spectacles. A ten-man Human Relations Committee was formed jointly by the union and companies in the industry. The committee meets from time to time on mutual labor problems. In June, 1963, this management-labor team announced that after five and one-half months of informal talks, rather than formal negotiations, an agreement on a new contract had been reached. The agreement was to run until May 1, 1965. This was a history-making development that gives hope that a new era may be at hand in the steel industry's employee relations. The agreement, which carried no wage increase or large increases in benefits, reflected recognition by steel union leaders of the existing economic situation in the industry.

7

The Problems of a Great Industry

WHEN I began my work for the steel industry in 1933, an old era was dying and a new one was dawning. The towering figures who had been managing the companies and building a great industry in accordance with principles they considered sound and lasting were never again to have the freedom of decision and action they had held so dear.

Some were embittered, but most accepted the facts of life and strove to adjust to the bewildering social and political tides that swirled around them. However, one by one the titans I saw on the Board of American Iron and Steel Institute in the early thirties gradually disappeared from the scene.

Their places were taken by men trained in the new ways of the oncoming era—men attuned to revolutionary changes within the industry itself and in all of the elements affecting the climate in which the industry operates. It is fortunate that the leaders of this generation have had this preparation because, as compared with their predecessors of thirty years ago, they are guiding a new industry in a new world. In sheer size of plant, in total investment, in competitive conditions, in new steels, and in labor and government relations, profound evolutions have occurred.

These changes have developed managements with new and added dimensions in leadership—dimensions that of necessity include a capacity for public affairs and public relations. Managements today must not only be competent to make sound business judgments. They must be prepared, just as is any public officeholder, to explain and defend many of their decisions to the groups that comprise their constituents; namely, the shareholders, suppliers, consumers, employees, and people in plant communities. Quite often, as well, they must face the general public. These things are true not only in steel but throughout all industry.

Tough public relations problems that were beginning to make their unwelcome presence felt in industry during the thirties have multiplied and grown tougher and more pervasive with the years. The steel companies have undergone some searing experiences during the past decade. Two Presidents of the United States have taken to the airways to administer wrathful attacks upon leaders in the nation's steel industry. What brought on these extraordinary performances?

The issue was basically identical in each case; namely, the right of managements in a free economy to make decisions vitally affecting the welfare of their companies.

We have seen in the preceding chapter what followed the Truman blast in 1952. Our firm was in the thick of that historic struggle, because we were retained by the group of companies involved. But in April, 1962 when President Kennedy attacked the steel price increases that had been separately announced by a number of individual companies, we had no part in the drama. In price matters each company is on its own, and we are employed by no individual steel company.

Needless to say, however, my associates and I were deeply

interested observers of the unfolding events. We were quite aware that in the face of four advances in steel-company employment costs since 1958, there had been no increase at all in steel prices. This was having a pincers effect on profits which had placed the industry in a serious dilemma. A price rise seemed to some companies the only solution. Following the Kennedy attack, we could see critical public relations problems building up for the steel industry, but very soon it became clear that these were being matched by the public relations problems the Administration had created for itself.

When competitive developments within the industry caused the price increases announced by a few companies to be revoked, it was called a "victory" for the Administration. But it was an outcome with enormously disturbing side effects for the national economy. The President's harsh words and the coercive moves against the steel men startled the entire business community. The Justice Department, Defense Department, Labor Department, Federal Trade Commission, members of the White House staff, and Administration-inspired Senate and House committees headed by Senator Kefauver and Representative Celler all moved together to intimidate and threaten the industry. Mr. Blough observed in an article, as told to Eleanor Harris, in *Look* magazine of January 27, 1963: "Never before in the nation's history had so many forces of the Federal Government been marshaled against a single American industry."

Business and financial confidence, already hesitant, went into a state of shock. Rightly or wrongly, the attack on steel was credited with having triggered the stock market collapse on May 28, the worst since 1929. Share prices, of course, had been drifting downward for a number of months.

The Administration began to take hurried steps in an effort to repair the damage. Various conciliatory moves and statements were made toward business. While the steel people had been deeply affronted by the assault upon them, it was crystal clear that no one either in government or management had anything to gain from continuing warfare between the administration and business. Roger Blough, Tom Patton and other steel leaders asserted their strong belief in the need for an understanding between government and industry.

In the article in *Look* magazine, Mr. Blough, recalling the intemperate remarks of Mr. Kennedy in "what was probably the strongest attack on a private industry ever made by a President," said:

> I decided on a tempered answer, although it would have relieved a lot of tension and frustration if I had yielded to natural impulses . . . But that is not my way. I was sure that an angry answer would only deepen the rift between government and business which was already so apparent. A tempered answer I felt would be more useful to the United States and everyone, including industry.

Mr. Patton, addressing the General Meeting of American Iron and Steel Institute one month after the President's attack, declared:

> We simply want to get on with our jobs under conditions which give us a fair chance to do them with success—and these conditions, I repeat, can only exist if government and industry have mutual respect for each other, and if, and only if, we have in this country a business climate that will enable us to hold costs in line, improve profitability and meet competition from whatever source it comes.

The right of businessmen to make their own decisions and their own mistakes, if need be, is inherent in the concept of a free economy. After all, the directives of government do not create wealth or jobs; these flow from the dynamic energies of many people at work in the complex interplay of the price, wage, and profit system. If competitive conditions are not such as to support higher prices, then they will be corrected naturally in the market place without benefit of government pressure.

Although many businessmen in America hold the view that the government's proper role in the economy is that of an impartial referee, others have come to accept intervention as the government's right and responsibility. Very few, if any, however, agree that government should use coercion and strong-arm methods to implement views not covered by the laws of Congress. One thing businessmen have learned from these and other events is that the executive branch of the government will be looking over their shoulders when important issues arise—that henceforth management will have added to the internal pressures it must contend with, terrific external pressures as well.

What the problem comes down to is whether, within the scope of fair regulations, management is to be free to manage. This means that in order to command enough profits to maintain and expand the industrial plant, prices must be set and employment and other costs must be kept under control. These are issues that in the end will be decided by the people, and it is of enormous importance that the people recognize what is involved.

As Roger Blough observed in his *Look* article:

> I am convinced that pricing by political pressure, rather than pricing by the forces exerted in a free competitive market, weakens the industrial strength upon which America's very survival may depend in time of crisis.

These are some of the reflections that worried many a businessman in America in the spring of 1962 and helped create a feeling of widespread uneasiness.

Meanwhile, as the administration considered the results of its action, the steel industry was viewing the situation from its own standpoint. Fortunately there were reassuring evidences that the Presidential attack had not undone, to any measurable degree at least, the effect of many years of public relations effort by the industry. Moreover, the incident brought public relations advantages to the industry. It brought more widely to public attention some of the acute problems facing the industry such as the profits squeeze and mounting foreign competition.

Steel was one of the first major industries in America to organize a broad public relations activity. The program began in an atmosphere of conflict and crisis, as have so many public relations programs. But, while much of the effort was devoted to extinguishing public relations fires, even at the outset, the program was centered on making facts about the industry available to the public and especially to leaders and molders of public opinion.

Thus, over the years, the effort has been to build up an increasingly deep reservoir of informed public opinion about the fundamentals of this great industry that has served America so well in peace and war. It was important that the people know about the great strides steel has made in production methods, in research, and above all in the creation of new steels that have added so much to the comfort and safety of everyday living.

The long-range benefits of these continuing efforts were evident in the generally favorable public attitudes as revealed toward steel when the smoke of the April, 1962 price incident had cleared away. Moreover, it became apparent that some part at least of the industry's message had gotten through to the Administration in Washington when in mid-April, 1963 price advances were announced by various companies for selected steel items. The White House reaction was dramatically different from that of one year before. Instead of blasting the companies, President Kennedy commended them for exercising "some restraint" and said the pattern "represented about a one per cent increase for steel products."

But at the same time he warned the industry against a price increase that would aggravate its "competitive position" and be against "their enlightened self-interest." He made it clear that he would oppose "across the board" increases while nodding approval for "selective increases" prompted by changes in supply and demand.

This development revealed a marked and welcome change in the bitter attitude of the Administration compared with the previous April. Yet it had ominous overtones. First there was the implication that Washington knew better how to set steel prices than long-experienced company managements. Secondly, there was the assumption that the President had the legal and moral right to tell the steel industry, or any other, just when, where, and how to price its products.

Obviously there is no statutory sanction for such procedure—but how about the sanction of public opinion? This is a disturbing public relations problem that has emerged for the steel industry and others as well.

If steel or any other industry is not allowed to go to the market in an effort to repair its thinning profit margins, then the free economy has ceased to function and we have no alternative but to go to a general system of price controls.

It is of tremendous importance that today's steel leaders are well aware of the industry's never-ending public relations problems and accept the responsibility for an unceasing public relations activity not only for their individual companies but for the industry as well. In American Iron and Steel Institute the industrywide program is under the overall guidance of a Public Relations Policy Committee, consisting of six board members.

They are Thomas F. Patton, chairman of the Institute and president of Republic Steel Corporation; Leslie B. Worthington, president of United States Steel Corporation; Arthur B. Homer, chairman of Bethlehem Steel Company; Charles M. Beegley, chairman of Jones & Laughlin Steel Corporation; Logan T. Johnston, president of Armco Steel Corporation; and Frank R. Palmer, chairman of Carpenter Steel Company. Most of these men have been through the crucible of public relations fires over the years. As a result they face their problems realistically. Said Tom Patton in a speech before a meeting of world bankers in New York City on September 24, 1962:

> Surely, we in steel have learned that there is still much misunderstanding among the public and their governmental officials as to our industry's needs and motives. We cannot automatically absolve ourselves of at least a portion of the blame for this misunderstanding. Our very closeness to our industry's problems has probably led us into overrating the degree to which others appreciate them and recognize their stake in the solution of those problems.
>
> American business today needs a fighting chance to conduct its affairs in an environment that encourages private enterprise and initiative. It needs laws covering its bargaining with labor that are fair and equitable. And it needs tax laws and depreciation allowances that are reasonable and realistic.
>
> Government has within its power the ability to do serious harm to the economy when its actions toward the business segment are rooted in mistrust and misinformation. But like it or not, the Government is unlikely to forego the exercise of considerable influence in the economic life of the nation. And if the Government has a responsibility to the nation to formulate intelligent fiscal policies and to provide a political

> climate in which private business is encouraged, so, too, is the business community obligated to conduct sincere and open-minded two-way communications with Government leaders with regard to economic problems and their solutions.

Still later at the General Meeting of American Iron and Steel Institute in May, 1963, Mr. Patton was able to affirm that "it is encouraging to note that in the past year there has been demonstrated a greater awareness" in both the executive and legislative branches of the Federal government of industry's problems. He cited the investment tax credit and the new depreciation guidelines as concrete indications of this growing government awareness.

It is in this spirit and with these objectives in mind that the steel industry conducts its public relations activities. What are the problems confronting steel that need wide recognition? These problems are legion, but three of the most outstanding of them may be outlined a follows:

1. Declining steel profits in recent years have been a threat to the companies' efforts to continue a healthy pace of modernization. The steel industry in America today stands first in all the world in its progressivism and I think most likely even in its modernization. The problem is to keep it that way.

But steel is a glaring example of the profit squeeze. Twelve years ago steel earned a profit of 8 per cent on sales and 15 per cent on net assets. In 1961 with a larger capacity, bigger output, and a greater population to serve, steel's earnings were down to 5.2 per cent on sales and to 6.4 per cent on net assets. The word "profits" has been denigrated into a bad word. Yet our country and our people live on business and business lives on profits—or dies. But changing the misconception about profits in the minds of the people cannot be done by "educating" them with abstract lessons in economics. Dramatic ways must be found to show how the contribution of profits—a profitable and prosperous economy—is vital to their personal well-being.

The steel companies have never ceased improving their properties when they had a shred of a chance. In the thirties they spent many hundreds of millions in the midst of the Depression to speed production, lower costs and improve products. Since World War II they have spent nearly 15 billion dollars in capital improvements. Now with ample productive capacity the industry's need is to spend money to achieve competitive costs.

2. In recent years sharply rising employment and other costs have been accompanied by lagging prices.

One of the never-ending public relations efforts in steel is to defog and debunk the clouds of misconceptions, and misunderstandings surrounding the industry. For example, I am always shocked when people speak of the conspiracy between the steel companies and the labor unions to raise wages and prices over the years. I have often heard this spoken of as though it were gospel. There is, of course, nothing to support such a statement.

The facts are all to the contrary. Since 1946 there have been seven industrywide strikes in the steel industry, five of them major. Although the "union shop" and other issues have been crucial at times, most of the major strikes were called by the union because the companies *refused* to yield to what they considered to be excessive and inflationary demands for wages and benefits. It is estimated that these strikes have cost the companies 10 billion dollars in lost production, to say nothing of the 3.5 billion dollars in wages lost to employees.

If the industry had been conspiring with the union to milk the American public, this surely was an odd way to go about it. Employment costs—wages and benefits—had advanced 173 per cent since 1947. Prices had gone up only 99 per cent. As of February, 1963, steel industry employment costs had risen by 18 per cent over what they were in September, 1958, the date of the last prior price increase.

3. Competition is mounting both from foreign steel and from other materials at home.

Today the industry is faced with terrific problems of competition. Employment costs in steel plants in this country are from three to seven times the rates paid in important foreign steel producing countries. Competition, as already noted, is coming from these countries as well as from other materials produced at home. Since 1950, American steel production has dropped from 47 per cent to 25 per cent of the world's total steel output. Although world production during that period has doubled, American steel output has increased only 1.2 per cent. But of course it remains true that with a steel capacity estimated at over 150 million tons of ingots, America stands head and shoulders above any other country in the world.

During World War II many steel plants in all the involved European countries were destroyed. These and others have been rebuilt in latest modern design, many of them with American-aid money. Japan also has a modern steel industry. The result is that now many foreign steel plants are approaching ours in efficiency with a far lower employment cost. Gradually over the years the wage gap may be decreased as foreign rates increase, but meanwhile we remain at a competitive disadvantage. In recent years the figures of rising steel imports and falling exports have told the dismal story.

In 1959, for the first time in more than half a century, the U.S. became a net importer of steel and that condition was continuing in 1962. But the overall steel import figures tell only part of the story. When the imports are broken down by major steel-product categories the real competitive threat to our steel companies becomes apparent. For example, in the first half of 1962, 46 per cent of the wire nails, 44 per cent of the barbed wire, 36 per cent of the wire rods, and 24 per cent of the concrete reinforcing bars used in this country came from foreign mills.

These, then, are three problems of vital importance to the steel industry. Obviously it is not within the competence of public relations to solve them. The solutions lie in lower costs, higher volumes, salesmanship, and other elements, but in order to achieve these goals managements need the support of better understanding by the public and by government at all levels. Having lived through the thirties when the steel industry was scraping bottom and having seen it emerge from the shadows miraculously stronger than ever before, I am sure that the difficulties of the sixties will also be surmounted, and by mid-1963 positive evidence of a turn for the better in steel had appeared.

Steel's public relations job sometimes seems more difficult than that of many other industries, and not only because it is inherently a big industry. More and more the American people are accepting bigness as a way of life in this age—bigness in business and in government. Steel suffers also from the fact that its product is wholly impersonal. The man who buys a new car, the woman who buys a new refrigerator, regards it lovingly as a Ford, a Chevrolet, or a Frigidaire and never stops to think that up to 80 per cent of this purchase is steel. To most of these people, steel is something big, remote, cold.

Just what does steel mean to me and my life? asks the average man. What does it do for me? And why should I worry my head about an industry that doesn't concern me? These questions are implicit in the attitudes of people and the industry is aware of them and is facing up to them. Steel companies know that they must identify themselves with the interests of people. They must humanize and they must dramatize their products and their industry and modernization plans. And they must make their problems familiar to people not in terms of steel company self-interest, but in terms of people's self-interest.

A dramatic effort to that end is the new steel industry exhibit at the Museum of Science and Industry in Chicago to which reference has been made in a previous chapter. There every year three million or more people from all fifty states and many foreign countries will come face to face with the wonders of steel—the metal that serves them so well.

An active, prosperous steel industry spreads benefits broadly throughout the land in jobs and in earnings. Moreover, steel provides safety and service to millions in their daily lives. To the extent that it is possible, the industry hopes to get this message directly to the people. However, in any effort of this kind it is well to recognize the existence of two major roadblocks. One is the appalling economic illiteracy prevalent in the United States. The other is the singular inability or unwillingness of countless numbers of individuals to absorb information unrelated to their daily lives.

For that reason a great deal of thought is devoted to opinion leaders; that nebulous and unnumbered group of men and women in America, who write, teach, preach, and in one way or another help to mold the attitudes of the people. Perhaps the most potentially powerful group for the spreading of sound economics exists in the large body of shareholders in American corporations. There are 17 million of these now and they have exerted little influence upon public affairs. Some day most likely they will be organized in the defense of their property and given a well-thought-out plan of action. When that day comes the shareholders could become an effective force.

In addition to its public relations activity in the realm of economics, the industry, also through the Institute, is carrying on a program to promote the use of steel products. A committee of top sales and marketing executives has been formed and, with various subcommittees and product committees, a major effort is being conducted.

During past periods of extraordinary demand the need to promote the greater use of steel was not always apparent. But in the recent years of severe competition, the industry has been taking energetic steps to find a way to the consumer's heart or at least to his intelligence. One useful device in this work has been to adopt a colorful symbol called "Steelmark" that is attached to millions of articles made of steel. The purpose, of course, is to remind people that modern steel has been used in the products to provide strength, durability, and economy.

Even though the Institute did not carry on a broad-scale product promotion program until recently, product publicity on a modest scale was part of the public relations program from the very start. When *Steel Facts* was to be started in 1934, I selected as my assistant John Mapes, now chairman of the executive committee of our firm, largely because he had had five years of experience in publicizing metal products.

Over the years both *Steel Facts* and *Steelways* have regularly carried stories on the advantages of steel. We also prepared several promotional booklets for the Institute before World War II. When product publicity and promotion was formally programmed in 1960, we assigned a team of specialists from our staff to the new program. They work under the direction of the Institute's Committee to Promote the Use of Steel, composed of top sales executives from the companies, and its Market Development Committee, made up of marketing experts.

I have recounted here the basic elements of the problems that in recent years have been confronting the steel industry —declining profits, rising costs, mounting competition, and the need for expanded markets. Against such a background is this overriding consideration: America must have a strong, modernized, and growing industrial plant—nothing must stunt the progress of any industry essential to our prosperity and to our defense. Steel is such an industry.

In this simple truism lies the heart of the public relations problem not only for steel, but for all basic industries. More than ever before, public understanding and support are needed by industry. The public relations problem is to convince the people and their representatives in government that strength and progress in industry are of benefit to all.

There are a few encouraging signs that some headway toward attainment of that goal has been made, but only increasing effort can hold and extend these gains in the years to come.

8

From Aircraft to Aerospace

IN September, 1943 my firm was retained by the Aeronautical Chamber of Commerce. The war was going full blast and the aircraft manufacturers were meeting President Roosevelt's "impossible" challenge to turn out 50,000 superior planes a year. That year they produced 85,000 and the next year 95,000.

Since shortly after Pearl Harbor, the Aeronautical Chamber had been playing a lesser role in representing the industry. When war came, the manufacturers did not feel that the Chamber was strong enough for the tremendous team job ahead; so they organized the Aircraft War Production Council. Well staffed and with highly active committees working regionally, the Council coordinated the efforts of the industry in war production. The manufacturers pooled their engineering and production data, their cherished secrets and know-how, and went all out to help swamp the Axis with air power.

For its purpose the Aircraft War Production Council was an excellent and dynamic organization, but it could not fill the need for a stronger voice, both for the remainder of the war and for the violent adjustments that would come with peace. Besides, the Council would have no place in peace. To continue it would constitute a conspiracy. It *had* to vanish with the last shot. The industry nevertheless would need a common voice and a common council when contract cancellations should begin. That was one of the lessons learned after World War I.

The first meeting of the Board of Governors of the Chamber after we had been retained was held in Los Angeles, and I was present. Then I made my first acquaintance with another group of rugged individualists. They included men who had founded great aviation companies bearing their names such as Glenn L. Martin, Donald W. Douglas, Sr., and Lawrence D. "Larry" Bell.

Present, too, were such pioneers as the late J. H. "Dutch" Kindelberger and Robert E. Gross, who took over the infant enterprises of North American Aviation, Inc. and Lockheed Aircraft Corporation respectively and built them into the great worldwide operations of today.

Other great leaders such as H. M. "Jack" Horner, chairman of United Aircraft Corporation; William M. Allen, president of the Boeing Company; J. S. McDonnell, chairman of McDonnell Aircraft Corporation, and Malcolm P. Ferguson of The Bendix Corporation were to come to the top in the next few years.

I learned at this first meeting that the companies felt the Chamber had been in a long decline and that it must be rejuvenated.

One thing was clear to me from the start and that was that the aircraft industry had a different and perhaps more difficult public relations problem than any other. Since the public was paying the bill for its product, the industry had more reason than most to keep the public informed about its affairs. Obviously, maintaining public confidence and goodwill was of the utmost importance if the industry was to continue to exist as private enterprise.

I particularly wanted the strongest public relations advisory committee that I could get. The Board agreed and the committee was named.

Shortly thereafter, a meeting of the new committee was held at the Yale Club in New York. About eighteen were in attendance and I was impressed by their caliber and stature. At that meeting were "Deac" Lyman of United Aircraft, John Canady of Lockheed, Lee Taylor of North American, "Rocky" Rochlen of Douglas, Ken Ellington of Republic, and others. Although I have formed warm and lasting friendships with many of these men, there was a chilliness in the room at that first session. Some were not enamored of the idea of an outside counsel. Others took a dim view of the fact that I had as one of my accounts an individual aircraft company, Consolidated-Vultee.

None of this came to issue in open meeting, but I was able to point out to a number of individual members privately the advantages of the broad range of services of our firm, which was already experienced in aircraft industry public relations. Also, for them to build an internal staff would be a long and doubtful process in wartime, and there wasn't time. The committee liked the outline of our recommended program; so the coolness disappeared and I never was aware of it again.

Our program benefited greatly from many suggestions by the committee. Only one sharp point of difference on technique developed. As one element of the Hill and Knowlton program, I had proposed that the Chamber issue a publication to be sent to opinion leaders in important categories. It was to be a sounding board for major public relations objectives of the Aeronautical Chamber, and it was to be somewhat along the lines of *Steel Facts*. The latter had proven a resounding success and had been used as a pattern by the automobile manufacturers in a publication called *Automobile Facts*.

We called the proposed publication *Planes*. I held that it should refer only to industrywide problems and achievements and never mention the name of any individual company. To do otherwise would be to invite a repetition of the competitive ill will experienced when the Chamber had issued an ill-fated clip-sheet featuring company names and accomplishments. I was surprised to find that several members of the committee disagreed with me. But I held my ground and finally won the point, and *Planes* (later renamed *Aerospace*) was created. For nearly twenty years this publication carried the industry's information to opinion leaders and, through the press, to the public. It has been widely quoted in the public prints.

The Aeronautical Chamber of Commerce had been formed by the manufacturers after World War I, but its doors were thrown open to almost everyone in any way connected with flying. In the thirties, however, the Chamber had become more and more of an industry association for the airframe and engine builders of America.

So the name "Chamber of Commerce" no longer was appropriate to the real purpose of the group. Consequently, we proposed that the name be changed. "All right," we were told, "but what should the new name be?" Our recommendation was that the name be made Aircraft Industries Association. This was done in 1945. Years later we were called on to consider another name change—when the scientific exploration of space took many of the industry's products beyond the atmosphere and the need of wings. Our suggestion was Aerospace Industries Association. The initials AIA were not disturbed, and "aerospace" is rapidly becoming a universal term. Many other aviation organizations have substituted it for aircraft in the new Space Age.

How wise the industry had been during the war in revitalizing its national organization became apparent at the end of the war when its survival was at stake. America began headlong disarmament. War machinery was scrapped. Sweeping cancellations of aircraft orders were put into effect. Production of military aircraft dropped from 95,272 in 1944 to 1,417 in 1946. In the same period, sales of the twelve leading airframe companies shrank from $5,766,000,000 to $519,000,000. Employment fell from 1,297,000 in 1944 to 238,000 in 1946.

Many thoughtful persons felt it would be disastrous, in the face of Russia's menacing attitude, for the United States to abandon its airpower. But the American people in great part were weary of war. They wanted their men home and they wanted to turn to peaceful pursuits. They assumed as a matter of course that the nation's defense planning and production should be drastically curtailed. How soon the painful lesson of Pearl Harbor had been forgotten!

The aircraft industry itself was deeply disturbed. Not only was its own existence in peril, but more importantly, it was convinced that the nation would be running a frightening risk to allow its air strength to evaporate. One articulate group wanted a nationwide campaign of advertising. The objective would be to jar the country out of its apathy about airpower. My firm was convinced that large sums should not be spent by the industry for this purpose, and we advised against it. We felt the problem was not one that was of concern to the aircraft makers alone, but to the whole country. A matter of national policy was involved and the need was for national leadership.

However, an industry committee was formed to develop advertising plans. After considerable study, a meeting was held in Chicago. The highlight of this meeting was a proposed program of radio commercials prepared by one of the country's large advertising agencies. The idea was that every few hours daily, on all significant radio stations in the country, there would be the sound of exploding bombs, followed by a bloodcurdling voice announcing that Hartford, or some other vital aircraft center, was being attacked by enemy planes.

After this holocaust had been depicted, the voice, now more calm, would explain that this was what *could* happen if the country were allowed to go unprotected in the air.

This medicine seemed a little strong. Fresh in memory was the time when Orson Welles had scared the wits out of the country with his too-realistic men-from-Mars program. The idea of such a radio program was dropped.

However, the problem remained and a good deal of study was being given to it. Eugene Wilson, former president of United Aircraft Corporation, was serving as head of AIA pending the selection of a permanent president. He recalled the enormously constructive contribution of the Morrow Board that had made a thorough study and evaluation of air power and the aircraft industry during the Billy Mitchell controversy of the 1920s. Wilson thought there ought to be a modern version, and he began to plant a seed that later was to grow into a highly contributory undertaking.

Wilson also requested us to develop a slogan. We asked all member companies to send in their suggestions. They did, and out of this long list the Public Relations Advisory Committee selected "Air Power is Peace Power." The Board adopted the slogan, we began to promote it, and it caught on. The United States Air Force took it as its own and made it internationally famous.

The aircraft industry was not alone in its alarm over the weakening of our air defenses and the atrophy of our industrial potential. The armed services looked gravely at the worsening conditions. More important, many congressional voices were expressing alarm and deep concern, beginning with Carl Vinson of Georgia, who has been Congress's foremost authority on defense for more than thirty years. Another was Senator Richard Russell, chairman of the powerful Senate Armed Services Committee.

The industry's convictions found expression in 1946 when AIA decided to establish its annual Williamsburg meetings, to which would be invited government and military officials for frank discussions of mutual problems. At this first meeting, Air Force and Navy uniformed and civil officials voiced their fears in strong terms. Our air power was facing extinction, they said, and they urged the industry to act to arouse Americans to the danger they were courting. They charged us to "do something to rescue the country, our air forces, and yourselves."

The AIA governors were deeply moved. They instructed the Public Relations Advisory Committee and public relations counsel to develop a program. This was done in twenty-four hours. The much expanded program was largely adopted by the Board and was promptly launched. It called for a virtual tripling of the annual public relations budget over the following two years.

Its elements were: intensified national and local publicity in support of legislation to set up a commission to study and devise an appropriate air policy for the country; an extended public speaking program by industry executives; cooperation with other national organizations to advance national defense and air power (such as the American Legion, VFW and labor unions in the industry); the preparation and distribution of printed communications to opinion leaders; cooperation with the Air Force and Navy in the distribution of films, publicity, and speeches; and providing congressmen with research and other information about industry and air power problems.

These and other steps were put in motion. In 1947 General Oliver Echols, who had retired as chief of procurement for the Air Force, was elected president of the AIA. General Echols was a man of few words, but they were always direct and to the point. He was single-minded and purposeful.

Bert Goss, as our account representative, was serving as director of public relations for AIA. He had compiled on one sheet some figures showing in graphic form the disastrous 1946 plunge into red ink of all the leading aircraft and engine companies. When General Echols saw this compact tabulation, he acted immediately to make sure it was given to officials of every member company. They were asked to hand it to every senator and congressman they knew and to other opinion leaders also.

Subsequently, the same figures were made available to the press. The *Washington Post* carried a front-page Sunday story summarizing these financial trends and saying that the survival of this vital industry was in question. Several weeks later, the *Washington Star* was to run a somewhat similar but larger story, more prominently displayed.

That afternoon, Senator Owen Brewster decided he would introduce the Air Policy Bill that the aircraft industry had been advocating. Next day, before noon, the Brewster Bill was introduced. A few weeks later it was passed and was combined with the Hinshaw Bill to create the Congressional Aviation Policy Board.

In the same month, July of 1947, President Truman appointed the Presidential Air Policy Commission—better known as the Finletter Commission after its chairman, Thomas K. Finletter. In the hearings before this group, the AIA witnesses were the chief executives of the aircraft industry. They did a splendid job—offering testimony, almost without duplication. They did not urge the government to buy more planes but simply presented a record of the facts and left the government to face up to those facts.

On January 1, 1948, the Commission issued its report under the grim title of "Survival in the Air Age." It called for a seventy-group Air Force (the then-existing force was thirty-four groups, only one or two equipped for combat) and commensurate increases in Navy Air.

Three months later, the Congressional Aviation Policy Board completed its hearings and came up with substantially the same conclusions.

The impact on Washington of these two reports was enormous. They were endorsed by thoughtful persons and major organizations the country over. Editors and columnists of the most important papers took up the cudgels to save our air power. Congress appropriated the funds to increase aircraft procurement and important programs of research and development. The aircraft industry, if not the nation, was pulled back from the brink of disaster.

During the big push for the Congressional Aviation Policy Board, there was a meeting of the AIA Board in Los Angeles. The Republicans, having won the Congress in the previous year, had made Senator Robert A. Taft the majority leader, and it was important to know how he felt on the issue of air power. It was decided that a delegation should see Senator Taft and this assignment was given to General Echols, Bert Goss, and me. We called the Senator's office and got an appointment for the following day.

As an admirer of Senator Taft I was enormously pleased at this opportunity to meet him face to face. I saw Senator Taft from time to time after that, and I never ceased to marvel at the penetrating clarity of his mind. People have called him cold, but to us that day, and always afterwards to me, he was cordial, warm and friendly. I noted that his desk, several chairs near it, and the window sills in the rear of it were all piled high with an array of books, pamphlets and government reports of every description.

He told us on this occasion that his own studies of the problem had convinced him that the country was making a tragic mistake in letting our air power deteriorate. He said he was all for a congressional study of the problem and would support it, which he did. He said he considered this cause of greater immediate importance than universal military training, an issue at that time.

As the Senator was bowing us out, I observed a large picture of his father making a campaign speech from the rear platform of a railroad train. I looked closely and remarked that I was sure I had heard that speech as a boy in 1908 in Shelbyville, Indiana. Senator Taft did not comment, but he gave me a smile of acknowledgment.

The AIA public relations program, from 1943 to 1949, represents the type of broad national campaign in the public interest that shows public relations at its best. No one can doubt that the AIA program and the two boards it supported played a large role in the adoption of the seventy-group Air Force program. When the Korean war came, our forces had a hard enough time as it was. If there had been no seventy-group Air Force program, there might not have been any industry to produce jet fighters. We might have been blown off the Korean peninsula without an air cover.

When Oliver Echols resigned in 1949 to accept the presidency of Northrop, Admiral DeWitt C. "Duke" Ramsey was elected president of AIA. He had been Chief of the Bureau of Aeronautics, Deputy Chief of Naval Operations, and had just retired as Commander in Chief of the Pacific. After nine years of service, he retired and was succeeded by General Orval R. Cook, former Deputy Chief of Staff, Materiel, of the Air Force. Both of these men were alive to the public relations problems of the industry and gave the work every encouragement and cooperation.

Although AIA public relations operations were less spectacular in the early fifties, despite the Korean war, they were active. Military aircraft production was doubled in the first year of the new decade and tripled in the third. Our jets in Korea rolled up a solid superiority of fourteen "kills" to one over the Russian MIG's. Exciting new weapons began to appear—great new jet bombers and fighters and guided missiles. The industry had recovered its strength.

But tranquillity is not for this dynamic industry for very long. On top of research, development, and production of aircraft and missiles came spacecraft. Ever since World War II, the aircraft industry had been dabbling with space, as much as skimpy budgets would allow. Only one non-military project had much of a priority or any substantial funding. That was Project Vanguard, intended to orbit a few grapefruit-sized, instrumented satellites during the International Geophysical Year, 1957–58. Even this undertaking was unhurried—and late.

Then on October 4, 1957—Sputnik! The shock of the Russian accomplishment had enormous public effect. Government reacted immediately. Major sections of the aeronautical industry went into high gear. Quickly we got some of our own satellites into orbit, and the race for space was on.

General Cook having retired, the Board of Governors of AIA selected a new president, Karl G. Harr, to guide its operations. A lawyer and a former Rhodes Scholar, with a number of years of experience in the White House and the Defense Department, Mr. Harr assumed his new duties in April, 1963, determined to help make the AIA an even more effective instrument of service to the industry and the public good.

The aerospace industry will continue to bear the hopes

of the nation for American superiority in space and for national security. Many billions of dollars are being invested in these programs each year. But this is by no means a prodigal industry. Congress keeps the industry under the lens of public scrutiny. Some elements of Congress would even deny manufacturers their patents and proprietary rights for commercial application of the fruits of their research and development. The General Accounting Office hovers over the industry like the FBI and Scotland Yard combined. Necessarily high costs are often mistaken for profligacy. In all, these and other pressures bear heavily upon aerospace industry profits that are usually far less than half the rate for all manufacturing. If the industry should, by some chance, make profits that are judged "too large," there is always the wringer of renegotiation to squeeze them out.

So serious has been the lack of understanding as these problems have mounted that AIA is conducting broad economic studies to help set the record straight. But the industry faces the constant need to meet public relations problems that are fully in proportion to the size and complexity of its operations.

Nowhere has private enterprise in this country reached finer flower than in the aerospace industry. Despite all the frustrations, harassments and economic crises it has encountered, the industry has managed to keep vibrantly alive and in front of the great advances in the sciences of air and space exploration. It has made great contributions to America's progress in the Space Age—progress that must be further accelerated in a world in which aerospace leadership is essential to the survival of freedom.

9

The Boy from Dayton

IN 1939 I met one of the most amazing men I ever have known—Victor Emanuel. He was president of the aggregation of companies that later became Avco Corporation, the control of which he recently had acquired from Errett Lobban Cord. Emanuel had a brilliant mind bordering on genius. He was a dreamer on a grand scale, a spinner of vast financial webs, a planner of large industrial empires. He and his company became my first industrial company client in New York, and my firm has continued in the capacity of public relations counsel for the organization throughout the intervening twenty-four years.

Emanuel was a true gentleman of the old school. He was genuinely courteous and took great joy in doing thoughtful things for others. Warm notes of thanks or of congratulations or of sympathy flowed endlessly from his office. At the same time, he kept many of his associates in a state of nervous exhaustion by expecting them to maintain the same killing pace at which he drove himself. Every day he sent a veritable barrage of voluminous letters, memoranda and miscellaneous reading matter to a long list of company officials and others.

He was inclined to shyness, which gave him an unjustified reputation as a "mystery man." Emanuel was one of the first executives to recognize the value of public relations and the importance of taking his public relations advisors into his confidence. He made this clear early in our relationship by inviting me to attend all meetings of the Board of Directors, and this has continued down the years.

He was born in Dayton, Ohio, and early joined his father in the utility business. In his late twenties, they had sold out to Insull and young Emanuel found himself with a fortune of nearly 40 million dollars. As a boy, Emanuel lived near the Wright brothers and saw them often. One of his boyhood friends was Earl "Red" Blaik, the celebrated football coach, who today is an officer and director of Avco. Another lifelong friend was Thomas O'Hara, who had been secretary to the elder Emanuel. O'Hara and Victor Emanuel became inseparable in business, the older man being a trusted counselor but never a paid official in any of the Emanuel companies.

After the sale to Insull, Emanuel went to live for some years in England where he rode to the hounds and was master of the famous Woodland Pytchley Hunt. But his fortune dwindled in the Great Depression and, when I met him, he was energetically trying to build it up again. Emanuel and F. D. Roosevelt were good personal friends, although they did not see eye-to-eye politically. FDR would call Emanuel to the White House for advice on his personal affairs. Emanuel often spoke of being with Mr. Roosevelt on several occasions when the President's mother would telephone her son about some phase of family finances. Then the whole manner and expression of the President of the United States and the Commander in Chief of the Armed Forces would change as he spoke to "Mama" and acquiesced in deferential tones to whatever she was telling him to do.

When the Japanese attacked Pearl Harbor and war broke out, Emanuel bought control of Consolidated Aircraft from Reuben Fleet. He already controlled Vultee Aircraft in Los Angeles and later the two operations were merged into Consolidated Vultee, the present Convair Division of General Dynamics Corporation. He asked Tom Girdler to run these companies and, in January, 1942, Girdler went to San Diego to assume charge. I went with him as public relations counsel. He spent one-half of his time there and continued to devote the other half to his job at Republic Steel.

Before going to San Diego, I was given a job about which I was none too happy. When Emanuel took control of Consolidated Vultee, he learned that the company, about a year before, had retained Steve Hannagan as public relations counsel. Girdler wanted me to take over the work because we had been together for years. I was asked to break the news to Steve that his contract would not be renewed by the new management.

I phoned him and made an appointment. I had met Steve some years before when, as a salesman for the Lord and Thomas Advertising Agency, he had called on me to solicit the American Iron and Steel Institute account. He had a breezy, winning personality with energy and drive. I imagine he suspected the nature of my visit but, when I arrived, he came to the reception room with a cordial welcome and escorted me to his office.

When I told Steve what the situation was, he said he quite understood and wished me luck. We parted on a friendly note. A few months later, however, he had his innings when he lured back into his fold a former employee of his I had taken over as our representative in San Diego. Tom Girdler had grown to like this man and he was unhappy with me for having lost him. But The Ford Motor Company had been given a contract to make Consolidated B-24s and they had retained Steve because of his experience with Consolidated. Quite logically, he went after his former employee and got him.

I never was to see Steve Hannagan again. He died in 1953 and control of his firm was taken over by William Robinson, who later became president of Coca-Cola. Robinson and George (*Presidents Who Have Known Me*) Allen had a mutual friend in President Eisenhower. Riding back north from Atlanta with the President one day in the spring of 1954, Robinson discussed his desire to sell his interest in the public relations firm. Allen advised him to get in touch with me. He did and, after some months of negotiations, we finally took over the old firm of Steve Hannagan. Hannagan was one of the greatest of all press agents, but made no claim to being a public relations man in its broadest sense.

The first public relations problem confronting me at Consolidated was to make the B-24, called the *Liberator*, better known. Emanuel and Girdler were irked by the fact that, whenever an effective Allied bombing raid occurred, the credit all went to the Flying Fortress, even if Liberators actually had been the bombers in the action.

I invited seventeen well-known newspapermen to come to San Diego to see the Consolidated Vultee plant. Among those who visited the plant were Turner Catledge, now managing editor of *The New York Times* and then of the *Times* Washington office; Frank Kent of the *Baltimore Sun Times*, and Richard Tregaskis of the *International News Service* who later achieved fame as author of "Guadalcanal Diary." They stayed four days and, on the last day, a battery of Army and Navy censors was on hand to clear on the spot all stories which had been written.

One writer didn't show up and I wasn't surprised because, much to my distress, he had nursed a bottle the whole time. I marked him off as a total loss, but got the most pleasant shock of my life when I returned East and found this writer's story prominently featured in his paper. It was an excellent and accurate report, and I never could understand how he had done it. The result of the trip was that, from that time on, the Liberator was no longer a forgotten airplane.

I shall never forget one memorable day in the summer of 1944 when FDR visited the Consolidated plant at San Diego. Thousands of people were lined up for a glimpse of the "War" President. As usual, the Secret Service had arranged for everything in advance. The President's car was to be driven into the main gate and then through the plant. Tom Girdler was told he would be expected to ride with the President and explain the plant to him. He was waiting for the President when he arrived and two of his top executives were standing beside him. They rather expected also to be invited to ride with the Chief Executive. But, as FDR came up, he spotted Tom Girdler and beckoned him alone into the car.

"They told me in Washington to watch out for you," Roosevelt said laughingly to Girdler as they drove off. I did not catch Girdler's answer, but I expect it was a good one, as he was never at a loss for words.

They drove through the plant with Girdler pointing out all the items of interest, including the "Mae Wests"—the protuberances on the front of the Convair seaplanes. Roosevelt was duly impressed with the Convair plant. He spoke of other aircraft operations and, according to Girdler, he said he had given Howard Hughes 18 million dollars to build a flying-boat transport, just on a hunch that something might come of it. "Maybe nothing will," Girdler quoted the President as saying. And nothing did.

I was at the spot where Girdler was to alight when the plant trip was finished. The car stopped, Girdler got out and the two men waved a stiff goodbye. Then Girdler began vigorously to scratch his chest and shoulders. I asked why, and he said:

"Before I got out of the car, he started scratching all over as though being with me had given him a rash. Dammit all, I think I have gotten a rash from him!"

When I went to San Diego on my first visit in January, 1942, Consolidated Vultee had 5,000 employees and one plant. Before the war was over, there were 100,000 employees and thirteen plants. Emanuel was proud of the fact that his companies were among the two or three largest producers during World War II.

It was my job to staff and direct the public relations departments at each of the thirteen plants. At the peak of the operation, I had seventy people scattered over the map of America, and the job of directing and supervising these distant and diffused staffs was not easy. I was frequently in the air going from place to place and, when in New York, on the telephone for long stretches of time. Obviously, I always was on the lookout for good people, and they were none too plentiful during the war.

One of our plants was at Forth Worth and I went there one day to settle a little difficulty in the public relations activity. I got the staff together and discussed the problem with them.

One of the staff, who was very young and very intelligent-looking, sat quietly at the back of the room for a while. Then, when the problem had been sufficiently confused, he started to speak—and, in a few minutes, introduced light and clarity into the meeting. I put his name—Kerryn King—in my notebook and, within a few months, I invited him to come to work with me in New York. He stayed in our organization for ten years, rising rapidly to become a senior vice president. Others noted his ability, too, and today he is vice president and assistant to the chairman of Texaco, Inc. and chairman of the Texaco Trinidad Oil Company.

One of the great achievements of Convair under Emanuel and Girdler was the development and building of the six-engine pusher plane, XB-36. I always shall remember the day in Fort Worth when I was cleared to see a wooden mock-up of this gigantic plane. It was truly breathtaking in sheer size. Nothing like this had ever been put into the air before. Some skeptics cast doubt on the success of the plane, but they were wrong. It was capable of delivering A-bombs anywhere in the world and was looked to, after the end of World War II, as the greatest single protector of America's safety before the coming of the long-range jet bomber, B-52.

As the end of the war approached, Emanuel began to worry about his large interest in Convair. He foresaw a collapse in the demand for aircraft and was disturbed about the future. He was increasingly annoyed that Girdler did not seem to share these concerns. Girdler had taken the Convair job as a war service and had no interest in the company's peacetime future. His heart was in Republic Steel, and he was anxious to get back at the helm in Cleveland when the Convair war job was ended.

Emanuel became so upset about the matter that he thought he should ask Girdler to give up the reins at Convair before the war was over. He talked to me at great length about the problem and I advised him to write a tactful letter to Girdler. In fact, I offered to draft such a letter for him. He said to go ahead. I handed it to him a few days later. I never knew whether or not he sent it. In any event, not long afterward Girdler called me in New York to come to see him. He wanted me to work on a statement of his resignation from Convair in 1945. While he seemed a little put out with Emanuel, I think he secretly was glad to be out of the bomber business and back full time at steelmaking.

Emanuel flirted with various schemes for keeping Convair on its feet after the war. One of them was a flying automobile. A large amount of money was spent in developing this idea, but it proved to be impractical. The contraption would work but it was neither a good automobile nor a good plane. Finally, in 1947, Emanuel decided to sell his interest in Convair to Floyd Odlum.

From making bombers he turned to making household appliances and running a broadcasting station, buying from Powel Crosley the Crosley Corporation and radio station WLW in Cincinnati. He also bought New Idea Inc., a farm equipment company. Later he acquired Bendix Home Appliances in South Bend.

At the end of the war, there was a huge pent-up demand for household appliances and this business went well for a number of years. But it declined in the fifties and Emanuel turned his brilliant creative powers to the building of a new empire in the world of advanced science and space.

Important to Emanuel in building virtually a new company after 1956 was the presence in the firm of two young men destined to move to the top two positions in Avco management. These were Kendrick R. Wilson, Jr., now chairman of the board and chief executive officer, and James R. Kerr, president and chief operating officer. They took their present titles after Emanuel's death in 1960, but they had major roles in shaping Avco's new character well before that time. Both are in their forties. Both have proved to be not only able administrators, but articulate spokesmen—a quality that has greatly aided in public relations for the company. Wilson, who came as a young man to Avco from Lehman Brothers, had worked on the company's affairs for some years previously and had won Emanuel's confidence. Kerr rapidly won recognition as one to whom long hours and long distances meant nothing. At one period he was commuting from New York to the West Coast twice a week.

Emanuel, a Cornell man, was a member of the University's Board of Trustees. Although he disliked parties generally, he rarely missed a reception for Cornell trustees and faculty members. One of these affairs that he attended in the fall of 1954 was fateful for his company and possibly for the defense of America.

At that time great difficulties were being encountered by the government in connection with its intercontinental ballistics missile program. This was largely due to the unsolved problem of "re-entry"—how to bring an ICBM warhead, enclosed in a nose cone, back from space through the earth's atmosphere without having it burn up as a meteor does. Emanuel was engaged in an animated discussion of this subject with a small group, when someone turned to him and said: "There's a man standing over there who can get the answer to that problem."

Emanuel immediately cornered the man and engaged him in a long conversation. His name was Dr. Arthur Kantrowitz, a Cornell professor of aeronautical engineering. He was also a world-famous authority on high temperature gas dynamics including the use of so-called shock tubes to simulate in a laboratory the same kinds of difficulties that would be encountered in an ICBM re-entry.

What Kantrowitz had to say fired Emanuel's always racing imagination and he set about trying to persuade the professor to join Avco. He was successful in this and from the chance meeting at the reception came a major development in Avco and in large measure the rapid solution of the ICBM re-entry problem. Kantrowitz, working with an outstanding cadre of scientists, found in record time the laboratory answers desired.

This achievement meant a great deal to Emanuel and to

Avco as it provided a sound public relations story at a time the company was emerging from heavy losses sustained in winding up the appliance business.

It was discovered that Avco's work with shock tubes held promise of capturing the public imagination. There is nothing very glamorous about a shock tube—it looks like a long pipe. What occurred inside the tube, however, was unbelievable, for this instrument was being used to produce speeds of thousands of miles an hour and temperatures as hot as those on the surface of the sun. In these shock tubes Avco scientists were duplicating, for fractions of a second, the same conditions that an ICBM would encounter when it reentered the earth's atmosphere. If the computations derived from the shock tube were correct, they would eliminate the enormously costly process of firing real ICBMs in a trial-and-error process to find an effective reentry vehicle.

Announcement of the shock tube work was made and generated wide interest in the press. Later a management decision by Avco to go ahead with the construction of a great, new scientific laboratory at Wilmington, Mass., near Boston, provided the continuing basis for a public relations program that in the course of the next few years was to help change the complexion of the company in the public mind.

A major public relations program was prepared for the dedication of this new facility in May, 1959. Attended by a host of distinguished scientists, governmental and civic leaders, it featured two important elements.

The first of these was a panel on the subject "Mankind and Space," with nine scientific participants including two Nobel Prize winners, and Bob Considine and John Daly as moderators.

Secondly came the unveiling of the first ICBM reentry vehicle to be recovered after a flight through space. This nose cone, for which Avco had developed the all-important protective material, was a dramatic sight. It was charred and blackened from its searing trip.

Coverage of the dedication was nationwide through press, radio and television. Proceedings of the scientific panel discussion were later summarized in a booklet that is still in demand.

Systematically, month after month, Avco continued to tell the story of its new work in science and space. However, five years were to pass before the general public truly understood the degree of Avco's change. In this period it emerged as leader in research and development of the Atlas, Titan and Minuteman nose cones—the "business end" of these vital deterrent weapons. Avco scientists scored breakthroughs that helped close the famous "missile gap"—and laid the foundation for a now acknowledged position at the forefront of the defense and space industry.

Today, Avco participates in more than thirty missile and space programs, including the Apollo lunar rocket. Nearly a quarter of its 27,000 employees consists of scientists, engineers and supporting personnel. Collectively they are a cross section of a new national breed in business, with a dual mission to preserve the security of the free world, and at the same time extend the frontiers of knowledge. They have brought about an era in which the impossible becomes the plausible and then the commonplace. Helping tell their story is a fascinating aspect of public relations.

But the company's research and development energies are not all devoted to the military and space. A large share of them are being channeled into the peacetime aspects of the business. And here, too, are fascinating stories to be told.

One important research project is a revolutionary method of generating electricity through magnetohydrodynamics. This resounding term is usually shortened to MHD. In the Avco MHD generator, a high-temperature ionized gas replaces the armature of a conventional generator and does away with much of the massive equipment associated with the present steam turbine generating system.

It is a challenging task to describe development in fields such as this to the general public as well as to the industrial community. Much interest was created, nevertheless, with the announcement that an output of 10,000 watts had been achieved from an experimental MHD generator developed in cooperation with a group of leading utility companies. Late in 1962 Avco announced that this output now exceeded 1,000,000 watts. MHD promises one day to provide generators 40 per cent more efficient than the most modern ones now being used. Russia and Japan also have shown keen interest in the system for their own utilities.

The boy from Dayton, who got his start in the public utility business, would have been pleased at this progress—and in the fruition of so many other of his dreams.

10

Operation Successful—the Patient Died

ONE bright and beautiful October morning in 1954 I was sitting in my office in a relaxed and happy mood. There had been no client crisis in a week and none appeared to be in the offing. I was looking out of the window contemplating some weekend riding on my horse through the trails and hills of Putnam County that now were at at the height of their autumn glory.

The telephone rang and the call I took smashed all my plans and plunged our firm headlong into one of the most exciting, intense and extensive battles of our experience. For nearly eighteen months we were in the middle of an often incredible drama that included in its list of actors the President of the United States, the Supreme Court, the Congress, an indignant South Dakota Senator, the man who telephoned me, and many others.

The man who called me was General Baird H. Markham. For many years before his retirement he had been active in the administration of the American Petroleum Institute and he was widely known and greatly respected throughout the oil industry. General Markham wanted to see me and we agreed on ten o'clock the next morning. When he arrived he was accompanied by Paul Hodges of Cities Service and two or three oil public relations men. He came to the point at once.

He asked me if we would be interested in doing a special job for the natural gas and oil industry. Explaining the nature of the proposed undertaking he said that it was the result of the Phillips decision of the Supreme Court in June of 1954. Prior to that decision, which had been a bombshell in the industry, oil and gas producers had always contended that they were exempt from regulation under the Natural Gas Act. But the Supreme Court surprised them and ordered the Federal Power Commission to regulate all producers who sold gas for shipment in interstate commerce. In substance, this affected almost all producers, large and small, throughout every nook and cranny of the oil fields.

The oil and gas companies regarded the Phillips decision as a catastrophe. They were proud of their record of supplying vastly increased supplies of gas at low prices. Under a competitive system free of regulation, the price of natural gas had risen far less than commodity and cost-of-living prices in general. For the consumer, it had been a bargain and had remained cheaper than competing fuels in most parts of the country.

Confronted with the need to do something about the Supreme Court decision, which put them under utility-like regulation, the oil and gas producers had decided that two steps were necessary. Believing that an informed public opinion will support sound measures in the public interest, the industry held that the first step was to take its case directly to the public. This would require a program on a national scale to inform the people of the issues involved and of the consequences of federal regulation.

The other step was to start a drive for legislation to terminate federal regulation of gas. It was decided that these activities had to be kept separate and distinct because of federal tax and lobbying laws. Accordingly, at the suggestion of M. J. Rathbone, then president, now chairman, of Standard Oil of New Jersey, the producers organized the Natural Gas and Oil Resources Committee to carry on the long-term information activity, and the General Gas Committee, an entirely separate organization, to help win legislation.

The Natural Gas and Oil Resources Committee was instructed to avoid scrupulously any involvement in lobbying, and this directive was rigidly adhered to under the always watchful eyes of the lawyers.

Shortly after the NGORC was set up with Leonard F. McCollum, president of Continental Oil as chairman, Paul Kayser, head of El Paso Natural Gas as vice chairman and James C. Donnell II, president of Marathon Oil (then Ohio Oil) as treasurer, General Markham was asked to take active charge of the operation with headquarters in New York. Although he was in retirement and enjoying a life of ease, the smell of coming battle and his close lifetime ties with the oil industry caused him to accept the emergency job.

As the work was to involve a large public relations operation, General Markham was faced with the need of finding a public relations firm with facilities adequate to the requirement. He was not familiar with the firms in this field and for guidance called a meeting of the senior public relations people of the major companies. Their verdict had been for Hill and Knowlton, Inc., and that explained the presence of the delegation in my office. I told General Markham and his associates that we would be glad to undertake the work. We shared their concern about the principles that were at stake.

Our first assignment was to develop a program that was to be presented at a meeting of industry executives in Chicago that November. We quickly put together a task force under the general supervision of Bert Goss, president of our firm, with John H. O'Connell, vice president, as account supervisor and a staff of Hill and Knowlton people that at one time included eighteen persons.

A comprehensive program of public relations was presented and this embraced a wide range of activities, including national advertising.

The basic element of this entire campaign was one of the most intensive mobilizations of an industry upon a nationwide scale that was ever put together. Under General Markham's direction the industry rapidly set up an organization consisting of fifteen regional chairmen and forty-eight state chairmen.

Although work actually was started only in October, by the first week in December a meeting of these regional and state chairmen was held in New York to launch a huge campaign reaching out into all the grass roots. At this meeting the state and regional chairmen were given a complete blueprint and a printed kit of materials for conducting a wide range of activities. The blueprint called for making contact with editors and publishers, arranging and making speeches before civic groups and other such audiences, showing of film on television and before other audiences, and other grass roots work.

The industry supplied General Markham with a large number of veteran and experienced oil company officials to work with Hill and Knowlton, Inc. in the preparation of all the needed materials, to supervise the vast range of activities and in general assist the 2,100 volunteer workers who came from all branches of the oil and gas industry.

Among the industry men who worked around the clock for months alongside Hill and Knowlton staff people were: Kirby E. Crenshaw, now president of the Cities Service Gas Company; Jack Raglin, then assistant to the president of

Continental Oil; Kenneth W. Rugh, manager, advertising and public relations for Phillips Petroleum; James M. Patterson, now director of public relations for American Oil; Kendall Beaton, veteran public relations man of Shell and author of a scholarly history of that company; Marshall B. Willis, director of advertising and publicity for El Paso Natural Gas; Russell D. Karns, assistant to the president of Standard of Indiana's producing subsidiary; and John Purnell of Cities Service. Many other company men came to New York for shorter periods of time.

It is almost impossible to detail the activities carried on in this nationwide mobilization. At one stage in the campaign, General Markham could report that there had been 1,718 favorable editorials as compared to 513 unfavorable and 210 classified as neutral. This editorial support reflected not only the distribution of an editorial information file to all editors in the country, but personal calls by dozens of oil and gas leaders.

Chairman McCollum and Vice Chairman Kayser personally headed the team of experts who called on editors and publishers of the leading papers in New York and Washington. In these meetings, editors were able to get authoritative comment on the controversial questions raised.

By September, 1955, just about midway in the campaign, NGORC and Hill and Knowlton reported that there had been 6,300 speeches and showings of a film called "You, the People." This film was also displayed 230 times on television.

The gas producers also reported that their case had been presented on sixty TV shows and 475 radio broadcasts. There had been by that time 2,400 contacts made with local chambers of commerce; 120 civic, municipal, and business organizations in thirty-four states adopted favorable resolutions opposing federal regulation of natural gas.

The Committee also sponsored advertising in newspapers

and magazines throughout various parts of the country. More than 2,000 volunteers from the industry participated in the overall program of public information.

The success of the industry's public relations campaign, and the legislative work the companies themselves carried on separately through the General Gas Committee and through their own facilities, can be measured in many ways. The opposition to the industry was formidable. It included virtually all of the city government officials in the United States. Working through the United States Conference of Mayors and the National Association of Municipal Law Officers, the city governments fought the oil and gas industry tooth and nail.

Organized labor and many professional consumer groups carried on bitter battles to preserve federal regulation. Various state utility commissions were also aggressive supporters of federal regulation. The oil and gas companies' principal customers—the gas public utilities—were mostly opposed to the producers.

All these opponents failed to acknowledge that existing low gas prices were the product of free competition, and many felt that the Federal government could hold down prices even in a period of inflation. The record since shows how wrong they were.

Yet in the face of this intense opposition, the campaign succeeded and the House of Representatives passed a bill exempting producers from regulation in 1955.

Early in 1956 the Senate began consideration of the bill. Then came one of the most incredible incidents in American history. The late Senator Case of South Dakota announced that two out-of-state lawyers representing an oil company (not a member of NGORC) had contributed $2,500 to his reelection campaign in apparent belief Case would support the Harris-Fulbright bill (to end regulation of gas producers). Case then announced he would reverse his stand and oppose the measure.

A major furor broke out in the Senate and spread to the country. Senators Fulbright and Monroney suggested the contribution might be a "plant." They and other senators demanded a sweeping probe.

Some senators contended that the vote on the bill should be deferred until the incident could be investigated. However, the leaders for both parties pushed for a vote and on February 6, the Fulbright bill passed by 53 to 38.

Thus, both Houses had completed action on a law exempting producers from regulation—a successful operation for the industry.

The Senate then unanimously adopted a bill creating a special committee to investigate the Case matter and Senator Case identified the lawyer-contributors. Neither lawyer was registered as a lobbyist and they represented an oil company that had *not* joined or supported either the industry's educational or its legislative committees (NGORC or the General Gas Committee).

Then came a new bombshell!

President Eisenhower vetoed the Harris-Fulbright Bill. In his message, he did suggest that Congress pass a new bill to exempt producers but with specific protection of the consumer. While thus supporting the principles of the vetoed bill, the President said he could not sign it until the pending probe was completed.

Because of the intense interest generated by the two lawyers' "lobbying" and the veto, a specially distinguished committee was appointed to conduct the probe. Naturally, the Senate's number-one prober, McClellan of Arkansas, was the chairman. The other Democratic members included Senators Anderson, Gore and Kennedy (now President). The Republican members were headed by Senator Bridges, minority leader, and also included Senators Thye, Purtell and Goldwater.

This special committee and its staff subjected our public relations program to a searching investigation and devoted two full days of public hearings to our program and the activities carried on. Attention naturally focused on the NGORC because of the well-publicized scope of our activities and because of our rigid avoidance of all lobbying activities.

These hearings thus provided one of the most comprehensive and detailed presentations of a public relations program that ever had become available to practitioners, college lecturers, or students interested in writing about actual public relations operations. But, of course, more important to us was the fact that the probe resulted in a complete clearance of our client, the NGORC, and of the Hill and Knowlton program carried out for NGORC.

In fact, at the end of two days of investigation, Chairman McClellan commented to reporters about the NGORC and its program: "In my opinion—and without the slightest suggestion that anything is wrong with it—the program it adopted might be calculated to have more influence on Congress than direct action."

And the *Washington Star* ran this headline:

"McClellan Calls Publicity Better than Lobbying."

There was one exchange during this investigation between the president of my firm and the senators that indicates how we operate in such a national campaign, and I believe some of it is worth reprinting here:

> MR. FAY (Counsel to the Senate Investigating Committee): Is it not true that a principle of your business of public relations is predicated on the fact that the constant presentation of ideas to the public through various media of com-

munication will, in time, establish patterns of thought and behavior?

MR. GOSS: We believe that if you give the people the facts, they will eventually operate on the basis of those facts, if you give it to them convincingly and effectively.

MR. FAY: Then it would be correct to say that public relations work is or can be an effective instrument which can be used to influence legislation?

MR. GOSS: In the sense that I just spoke, that the legislation is ultimately going to operate from a basis of the facts and the belief and opinions held by the people, yes.

MR. FAY: Would it also be fair to say that if you had literally unlimited funds available to you to press for any particular concept or regulation, using the regulatory field, that you could effectively as a public-relations firm put across such legislation if it was not basically vicious or evil?

MR. GOSS: The task of trying to inform public opinion is a very complex and a very difficult job. It does take a day-in-and-day-out job. So just the possession of money alone won't do it. There are many other aspects of public-relations activities that do not require particularly out-of-pocket expenditures at all, and they are very important and they are available to other groups in society as compared to business.

There are the unions and the farmers. They have tremendous public-relations power, let us say, because of their membership and because of their grassroots strength, and it does not stem from money. You cannot just simply say the possession of money would enable you to carry on a public-relations campaign that surely would change public opinion.

Money is, of course, important, but there are many strengths that you have to draw upon, which we drew upon in this activity, that do not stem directly from money.

If the oil and gas industry was not doing a good job in their own plant communities all over America, and if they were not well-respected citizens, and if they did not have very sound community-relations programs which do not stem from the expenditure of money for newspaper advertising or publicity but just results from being a good citizen —I doubt very much that the expenditure of a lot of money would have any appreciable effect on public opinion at all.

The general nature of the NGORC program was emphasized by Chairman McCollum of Continental Oil Company, in his closing presentation to the Senate Investigating Committee. He said:

> Our various advertisements and pieces of material outlining our case are here for your examination. We believe we have carried on an information and education program that is direct and honest. We expect to continue such a program. I say this because any industry that believes in its case would be derelict in its duty to its shareholders and to the public if it did not tell its story fully and clearly to the American people.
>
> It is imperative that there be the fullest possible dissemination of information and the freest possible debate over any basic economic issue that confronts the Nation. Any official moves to limit, directly or indirectly, the distribution of information about such basic economic issues would therefore be a serious danger to our form of Government.
>
> In fact, I should like to recommend that the Congress should do everything in its power to encourage rather than discourage, programs of this type. This recommendation, of course, applies just as much to those who oppose our views as it does to us.

Looking back over this effort, oil and gas producers can take considerable pride in the activity carried on.

For one thing the entire campaign was subjected to a merciless investigation and not a single wrongful or improper act was disclosed.

More importantly, subsequent events have fully justified the contentions NGORC advanced in its battle to exempt producers from regulation. The Federal Power Commission has remained bogged down in its effort to regulate natural gas, just as NGORC predicted. The burdens of federal regulation have proved harassing, costly and impossible, particlarly to the small producers.

The cost of natural gas to the consumer continued to rise under federal regulation, and perhaps at even a more rapid rate than had occurred when producers were free of such regulation.

All of this was repeatedly forecast by NGORC in its fight against controls.

Even more heartening has been the change in attitude of the gas utilities that distribute the product directly to the consumer. These utility companies subsequently discovered that federal regulation was hopeless and undesirable. In recent years they have been working with the oil and gas producers in an effort to develop legislation exempting producers from regulation. This action is one more evidence that the campaign was sound and that it truly represented an effort in the public interest as NGORC contended.

11

The Role of Public Relations Counsel

IN my early days in public relations, the work was concerned chiefly with press relations. Since then it has come to cover a wide range of activities bearing upon all phases of communications. Press relations, of course, continue to be important but there are many other kinds of relations. There are relations with customers, with employees, with government, with stockholders, with people in plant communities, with educators, and with other groups. The public relations counsel must be prepared to provide advice and active help in any of these categories as the needs arise. He cannot properly speak for a client unless requested and authorized to do so.

In my view the basic role of public relations counsel is to give *counsel* to his clients, based on wide and varied experience. But, it may properly be asked, counsel on what? Public relations counsel are not lawyers. They are not management engineers. They are not sales specialists. They are not labor relations experts. They are not scientists. They are not certified public accountants. Then on what do they counsel? Curiously enough the recommendations for which they are asked in one way or another may impinge on any of these fields. Perhaps I could clarify this by giving at random a sampling of the problems put to our firm week in and week out, for which we are asked to find or to help find the answers.

1. A billion-dollar company is thinking of changing its name. Will we study this problem and recommend whether this should be done and, if so, what the public relations advantages would be and what new name would we suggest?

2. The products of a large industry are being attacked on the grounds of health. What should be done to meet the situation?

3. An important company is faced with an antitrust suit. What, if anything, should be done in cooperation with legal counsel to protect its good name and insure understanding of the company's case?

4. An industry is denounced by a high government official. What kind of a public relations program, if any, is called for to meet this problem?

5. An industry is hailed before a hostile congressional investigating committee. How can unfair charges be countered?

6. A large company in an African country is accused of wrongfully paying taxes to a local de facto government. How can it be made clear that this company has no choice in the matter—that no one is free to choose his own tax collector? Either pay taxes to the local authorities or face certain confiscation.

7. Two companies in a public service industry want to merge in order to gain efficiencies that will enable them to survive and improve their service. How can public understanding of the importance of the proposed merger best be obtained?

8. A privately owned company plans to "go public"

issuing stock and other securities. What steps can and should the company take to inform analysts, prospective investors, and the financial community generally about its prospects for growth and profitable operations?

9. A company that must adopt technological advances to remain competitive finds these advances understandably opposed by employees who fear that their jobs may be endangered. In addition to taking all possible operating steps to protect the employees' security, how can management most effectively show the employees and the community the vital necessity of the changes?

10. A materials-supplying industry wants to sponsor a research program that will benefit its customers. What kind of research would be most useful and what organization or educational institution should conduct it?

11. A manufacturing company has an important news announcement of interest to the financial district, customer industries, and the government. What form should the announcement take—press conferences in several cities, special releases to various interested media, or in-person contacts?

12. A large industry association is undertaking publicity promotion programs for a number of important product groups. What is the most effective plan or plans for carrying out these programs?

13. A company confronts an organizing drive by an international union known for militancy and violent strikes and disturbances. What can the company do to alert employees to their stake in responsible labor relations?

14. A large industry is facing a demand for increased regulations during a time of widespread criticism of some of its products—should it "go along" or fight the legislation?

15. A large company nears its one-hundredth anniversary. Can a celebration of this event be so conducted as to help product sales and company public relations?

16. A company in the international field wants to make its name known in the European Common Market countries. What kind of program should be devised to meet this problem? What groups are most important and how can they best be informed?

17. A company has a problem relating to financing. What is the way to proceed with public announcements in keeping with the publicity requirements of the SEC?

18. A company is being threatened with boycott by Negro groups because of alleged discrimination in employment. What steps can be taken to meet this problem?

It is obvious from this random list that the problems coming to a public relations counsel simply reflect the range of problems confronting management in our complex modern society—a society in which public attitudes play a vital role. Communications are inherent in many of these problems. Included also are the public relations aspects of economics, political science, medical research, finance, accounting, labor negotiations, antitrust suits, management, international trade, education, sales promotion and other fields.

More and more it is becoming important for every well-rounded public relations firm to have on its rolls people who have equipped themselves with some knowledge of one or more of these specialized subjects, not in the sense of giving final answers, but in at least knowing where and how to get those answers. And, of course, there is the need for basic skills in the art of informing public opinion.

Lawyers can cite statutes, judicial precedents, and established legal procedures in arriving at their advice and counsel to clients. Public relations people in the main must rest their counsel on experience plus opinions and judgment that are binding on no one. What is the role of public relations counsel in dealing with these matters? I have attempted in this book to describe in some detail a number of problems and the methods employed in meeting them. But in general let me say that counseling on public relations calls for a variety of special experiences, abilities, and qualifications. In my opinion the most important single element is integrity, which is a matter of character. Next to integrity I would rank judgment.

You can teach a man many things, but how can you teach him to exercise judgment? An accumulation of experience will help, but nature must have laid the groundwork. Many a public relations man, competent in all phases of the work, has come a cropper because of lack of judgment. Judgment is an elusive element that usually refuses to make known its presence or absence until a crucial moment arrives. Only by consistently displaying sound judgment in these moments does the man who possesses it distinguish himself.

The well-rounded public relations counseling firm of today plays a flexible role. It may be asked to assume the sole responsibility for the public relations work of a company or an industry association as we do in some cases. It may be retained to provide counsel and operating assistance to a client or counseling exclusively.

Many corporations have public relations staff officers and, at the same time, avail themselves of the independent viewpoint and facilities of counseling firms. The role of a counseling organization may be described as follows:

1. It provides objective counsel—advice uncolored by any subjective problems that may exist within the business.

2. It provides a diversity of experience in dealing with a multitude of public relations problems.

3. It gives client companies access to services, facilities and the various specialists in phases of public relations, thus enabling the client to supplement its own staff operation.

4. It gives an outside viewpoint on probable public reaction to company policies and acts.

5. It underwrites with its own reputation the quality and continuity of the undertaking.

Some companies think of human or public relations in terms only of talking to others, forgetting the need to *listen* as well. It is just as important for company management to understand the problems and viewpoints of its employees, neighbors, and others as it is for these groups to understand the problems and viewpoints of management.

Without this kind of understanding on the part of management, policy thinking and communications will lack the human touch. It is an essential function of the public relations counsel to serve as a listening post for management—to help it appraise other reactions and viewpoints. Some managements may not like this aspect of public relations, but most welcome it and profit from it.

Typical of the questions that need to be answered before a sound public relations program can be constructed for a corporation are these:

1. How sound and stable are its relations with employees—and what do employees think about the company?

2. How are relations with customers, distributors, dealers—and what do they think of the company?

3. How are relations with stockholders and the financial community—and what is the opinion in those quarters about the company?

4. How does the company stand with prevailing public opinion in the communities where its plants are located—and to what extent does it assume its share of community responsibility?

5. Does the company have any problems with governments—federal, state, or local—and are these legislative or otherwise?

6. Does management have adequate and effective ways of communicating in person or by other means with its em-

ployees and with all other groups with which it has relationships?

7. Are key personnel informed sufficiently about company affairs—are they able to explain and defend broad company policies to employees and others?

8. Is there a well-thought-out and workable plan for responding to the many appeals by worthy causes for company contributions?

9. Is there a plan for cooperating with educators in supplying them with factual material for school use as desired?

10. Are members of management sufficiently articulate in explaining their own business and the workings of the enterprise system when occasion demands—and is the company benefiting enough from leadership by management in public and industry affairs?

11. Are the company's achievements and products sufficiently known to its public and is there need for improving goodwill?

12. Are press relations good, bad, or indifferent?

To some people, the scope of this line of inquiry may seem too broad for their more restricted idea of public relations. But the truth is that the interest of public relations extends to every aspect of management and of the business where goodwill may be affected or at stake.

After all of the twelve questions just listed—and often many more—have been answered and the management policies clarified, a public relations program may be developed.

The scope of the program depends upon the scope of the operations of the enterprise and the various segments of the public it wants to reach. Ours is a vast and complex population of 189 million people, many of whom are indifferent to remote corporations and some of whom are antagonistic toward them. To try to reach the whole public in all its components is a gigantic undertaking, calling for consistent use of every avenue and technique of communications through the printed and spoken word.

Sometimes, of course, intense human-interest issues arise that place companies or whole industries in the spotlight of nationwide attention and debate. Here the question of communications often involves the need to get a fair hearing in an atmosphere charged with clamor and emotion.

On this score, critics of business have nurtured one rather ironic fallacy that shows itself as a major public relations problem from time to time. That is the unsupportable but recurrent notion that businessmen should not speak up on behalf of their companies or industries when they are under attack, especially if the attack comes from educational, scientific, or even governmental sources.

It has always been my belief—shared, I think, by most Americans—that every man has a right to a hearing, and if he is under public attack, the right to defend himself publicly.

As the complexities of public relations problems have increased, the role of public relations counsel and the numbers of people in this field also have expanded. And it must be acknowledged that, while the public relations counseling field has grown in quantity, it has shown something less than a uniform growth in quality. The same, however, could be said of any other profession or vocational field. I am sure that lawyers and doctors are tired of being reminded that there are shysters and quacks and inept people in their ranks, but it is a visible fact that *every* occupation has its share of incompetents and charlatans.

The public relations counseling field is comprised largely of practitioners with sound ethical standards. But unfortunately it must suffer the blanket criticisms brought on by those who are the exceptions. All too often the ethical and capable practitioners find themselves wincing under the news of some shady or stupid act committed by an irresponsible operator who has hung out a shingle announcing that he is a public relations counselor.

Earnest efforts have been made to develop a workable and enforceable code of ethics for the public relations counseling field. There are some areas in which it should be possible to achieve constructive results, but I fear they will be limited. Unlike law or medicine, public relations cannot be defined in precise terms. The term has been brought into use to cover a multitude of activities, many of which are wholly unrelated. A Washington lobbyist or "influence peddler," a specialist in getting names mentioned in society gossip columns, a night club press agent, and dozens of others all may have a shingle on their doors reading "public relations," as they have a perfect right to do if they want it. The task of prescribing ethical boundaries for all of the heterogeneous activities bearing the label of "public relations" is impractical, to say the least. There are some who advocate a system of state licensing under which certificates to practice would be issued only to those applicants who passed an examination. I am convinced that no such examination with any meaning whatsoever could be developed in the foreseeable future.

I believe the greatest hope for the future of public relations counseling lies in the fact that the number of strong responsible firms is increasing year by year. These firms must set the pace and lead the way in establishing ethical standards and sound practices. To the small extent that a code can help in this, all well and good, but the example set by the leading firms will prove of major importance in achieving desired public recognition.

One practice which I believe should be eliminated is that of the so-called "paper front." A client is advised to finance an "organization" to promote or fight for its cause under the guise of an independent and spontaneous movement. This is a plain public deceit and fraud and of course is a technique developed with consummate skill and in great profusion by the Communists. In a free country any interest with a cause has a right to present its case to the public, to inform and, if possible, to persuade to its heart's content. But that right of free speech also carries the obligation that the source of it will be in the open for all to see. Attempts to fool the public by making it believe an "organization" existing only on paper is really a vociferous group favoring this or that cause have helped to cast a shadow upon the business of public relations counseling. No counsel who wants to preserve his own reputation will ever be a party to the issuance of any public statement by a client unless the source is clearly set forth. Obviously, when a client is involved in a public relations controversy, supporting statements are welcomed from every responsible source. But such statements should be issued by real-live people or organizations and not phoneys.

Press relations usually is not the primary assignment given a public relations counsel. His first responsibility in virtually every instance is to assist the client in developing and carrying out an effective, long-term public relations program. Often a part of this program is to maintain good communications with the company's publics, a goal that can be accomplished adequately only if newsworthy information about the company appears in the public press.

Newspaper editors and reporters quite properly resent public relations counsel who attempt to stand between them and a client. In our firm in press relations we are concerned only that the information be properly available to the press and that it be authoritative, accurate and meaningful. It does not matter to us whether the reporter or editor gets it directly from the president of the company, the public relations director, or our own account executive. Certainly we have no objection to newsmen going directly to the company itself for information when they wish to do so; in fact, we quite frequently put them directly in contact with company people when they are seeking information that can best be supplied in that way. What is important is the communication itself, not the channel through which it gets into print.

The first step for counsel in the development of a public relations program for any organization is a study of its human relations and how these are affecting its total welfare. Progressive management knows that its human relations problems are just as specific and important to the company's business as are its other corporate responsibilities.

The extent to which the public relations counsel influences policy depends upon whether he can demonstrate capacity for giving sound, practical and objective advice on policy matters. If he can do so, there will be little question about his role in policy decisions. If the practitioner has something to offer, he is likely to get the opportunity. If he has no original or helpful ideas, he is not likely to get very far in policy deliberation.

My observations may seem to imply that only business and industry are concerned with public relations service and employ public relations counsel. Of course, this is not the case. Many other kinds of organizations and institutions maintain public relations activities, including labor unions and government bureaus. A candidate for Congress has written to the American Bar Association suggesting in all apparent seriousness that the United States Supreme Court retain public relations assistance to explain its decisions more effectively to the American people.

The Justices may not readily adopt this proposal, but the fact is that the roster of non-business organizations utilizing the public relations function is steadily expanding.

While my firm has been oriented toward work for private enterprise, we have been retained by governments and by various non-profit organizations. I am reminded of one day in the spring of 1955, when Roland Harriman and Ellsworth Bunker, chairman and president respectively of the American Red Cross, came to my office. They said they would like our firm to do some work for the Red Cross. I said we would be delighted to contribute some of our time and talent to such an outstandingly worthy cause.

"No," said Mr. Harriman, "we do not want volunteer work. We want to retain your firm on a regular commercial basis. We want the full service of your organization for a period of a few years. We need a thorough survey and evaluation of all that we are doing together with your public relations program recommendations." I felt very much flattered by this proposal and, of course, accepted the assignment.

We worked with the Red Cross for three years, during much of which time the organization was called on to aid the victims of a series of floods, hurricanes and other disasters. From crisis to crisis, my admiration grew for the unruffled patience and extraordinary skill with which Roland Harriman and Ellsworth Bunker administered the great Red Cross organization.

Edward W. Barrett, now Dean of the Columbia Graduate School of Journalism, was our firm's management supervisor of the account and he was assisted by Charles Hurd, formerly of *The New York Times* and more recently author of *The Compact History of The American Red Cross*. Our contribution was to study the national and local operations of the Red Cross and to devise a basic public relations program that could be assimilated and used by the 3,700 chapters of the organization. The program, as carried out, called for activity to concentrate on the broad publicizing of four basic themes: 1) the widespread range of services provided by the Red Cross; 2) the unique and official character of the Red Cross; 3) the indispensable nature of Red Cross services;

and 4) the Red Cross organization as a stand-by army for emergency rescue and aid missions.

By the time Mr. Bunker resigned to become Ambassador to India our work had been completed. The Red Cross was fortunate in getting as Mr. Bunker's successor, General Albert Gruenther, who assumed the presidency upon his retirement as the head of NATO in 1956. Since then General Gruenther has devoted his extraordinary abilities and boundless energy to this great organization.

When a company, an industry, or any significant organization wants to meet a specific, overriding public relations problem or to develop a more effective across-the-board public relations program, the guidance and experience of a sound public relations counseling firm usually can be of great help. The contribution of public relations counsel to the worldwide progress of business enterprise will continue to grow to the extent that the counseling field matches this opportunity with wise and farsighted effort.

12

Anatomy of a Public Relations Firm

DURING the years of my practice in public relations I have started three operations—the first, in Cleveland in 1927 was regional; the second, in New York in 1933 is national and international; and the third, in Geneva in 1954 is European. My chief concern in all of these firms was to staff them with people of ability. The importance of this is not hard to see when it is realized that a public relations counsel has nothing to sell but service.

I recognized from the outset that my company would be only as capable overall as the individual men and women I could assemble in it. In the early forties as the business expanded, I arrived at three basic conclusions, all of which pivoted upon the essentiality of competent people.

The first was that the need in public relations of the future would be for counseling organizations with a broad spectrum of services. The second was that, in order to be effective and workable, such an organization must be a team operation. This, it seemed to me, was sure to replace the lone-wolf operator—the "Big I Ams"—as an important factor in the public relations business. The third conclusion was that public relations was growing up as a business and should be run as one. I kept these goals constantly in mind and gradually worked toward them.

My first step toward building a staff in New York came with my move there from Cleveland to handle the American Iron and Steel Institute work. My first employee was J. Handley Wright, an able young man—now vice president of public relations for the Association of American Railroads—who came with me for a time. However, he got a much better offer and soon was gone. Then, one day in 1934, I had a piece of good fortune.

A tall, obviously competent and experienced young man from Cleveland came to see me. He had been director of public relations of the American Society for Metals, and assistant editor of *Metal Progress*, a national trade publication. I put him to work without delay and—except for a brief interlude—he has been a mainstay of our organization throughout the subsequent years. He is John G. Mapes, now chairman of the executive committee of Hill and Knowlton, Inc., and chief coordinator of all our work for the Steel Institute in addition to other responsibilities.

Another key man came into the organization in 1943 when our firm was retained by the Aeronautical Chamber of Commerce. The headquarters of the new client were in Washington, and I needed a responsible representative on the ground. When I asked John Mapes to find us a well qualified public relations man, he said he knew just the man, and in a day or two brought him to see me. I recognized him at once as the former business editor of *Newsweek* magazine, whom I had once met. His name was Bert C. Goss. Before going to *Newsweek*, he had taught economics, in which he had a doctorate, at New York University and had been an editor of the *Journal of Commerce*. He joined Hill and Knowlton, went to Washington for seven years, and is now president of our firm.

In 1952 Richard W. Darrow came with us from the Glenn L. Martin Company (now the Martin-Marietta Corporation) where he had been director of public relations and advertising. Behind him already at that time were eleven years of public relations executive experience and a number of years of newspaper work on metropolitan and some city dailies. Behind that was a record as a Phi Beta Kappa student at Ohio Wesleyan University. He is now our executive vice president and public relations chairman of the Boy Scouts of America.

In our management group also are five senior vice presidents: James J. Cassidy, formerly public relations director of Crosley Broadcasting Corporation; William A. Durbin, formerly director of public relations of the Burroughs Corporation and of American Cyanamid Co.; Paul J. Boxell, former journalist and English instructor at Indiana University; Vern M. Boxell, formerly city editor of the *Indianapolis Times* and aircraft public relations executive; and John H. O'Connell, formerly public relations director for companies in the aircraft and consumer goods fields. The average public relations experience of these senior vice presidents is twenty-one years.

The management group and other key staff members meet at necessary intervals to discuss client problems and to develop programs to meet client needs.

In building our staff far beyond the nucleus of these men, I consistently sought strong associates who could accept increasing responsibility. I felt, as the public relations problems of our clients multiplied and became more and more complex, that I did not know all the answers. I may also say that, in my wide acquaintance, I know of no single individual who does. Therefore, in building an organization I have aimed also for a variety of experience, education and talent. Our staff is comprised of men whose backgrounds cover wide-ranging facets of business, government service, teaching, science, financial analysis, newspaper and magazine editing and reporting, advertising, television, and publication graphics and production.

In 1963, we studied some statistics on our staff and learned, among other things, that:

1. Our average staff member was a man with fifteen years of experience in public relations. In the full officer group, the average was nineteen years.

2. Most of our account executives were formerly directors of public relations for a wide variety of industries and institutions.

3. More than three-fourths of the total staff had worked as editors, writers and reporters in twenty-three states, the District of Columbia, and eight foreign countries. A number were holders of special journalism awards.

4. Members of the firm had authored some forty-four books and had made prolific contributions to more than 100 publications and periodicals.

5. Of the twelve executives of the firm who qualified as teachers, ten had taught these subjects in colleges and universities: English, speech, psychology, finance, education, physics, and international relations. Three held Ph.D. degrees.

6. Several held law degrees.

7. Members of our staff in the United States, exclusive of our international subsidiary, had traveled or worked in ninety-seven countries on every continent. Thirty-three could read or write French, nineteen German, eighteen Spanish, three Russian, three Italian, and one each Arabic, Greek, and Dutch.

Only by such a variegated grouping of education, experience, talent, and linguistic capabilities can a large public relations firm meet the requirements of its clients.

As the business grew, changes also had to be made in our financial methods. The evolution, I am sure, was similar to that which had marked older fields of business on their way to maturity. For many years most public relations firms, including my own, operated in a rather haphazard financial fashion. My initial fee was set by my first client and this figure prevailed for some years. Then one of my important clients told me I was doing it all wrong. This became more and more clear to me, so one day I decided to employ Price Waterhouse to analyze our affairs and tell us how to put them on a business footing.

After some months, they came back with a plan that we adopted in the main and is still in effect. I believed that our clients would prefer doing business with an organization operated on a businesslike basis with standard fees and staff-time charges—and I was right. Since the product we have to sell consists altogether of time, talent and experience, I felt that the client should pay for this only to the extent he uses it. For this reason, every productive person in our employ is required to keep careful hour-by-hour time records.

Very early I also ruled against any solicitation of business. I felt that business executives of the caliber we liked to work for would not welcome high-pressure "selling" approaches. They are perfectly capable of deciding whether they want outside counsel and whom they want. I have witnessed many expressions of surprise from people when they learn we have no new-business department. "How could you grow to be such a large public relations firm without soliciting new clients?" they ask. My explanation is that we have tried over a period of three and one-half decades to build a reputation for high standards of service. My ambition never was to be the largest firm, but the best.

Looking back over those decades, I can count a number of innovations that our organization has pioneered in the counseling field. These include, among others:

1. Development of a broad range of specialized public relations services staffed by experts.

2. Establishment of systematic planning and execution of public relations programs for major industry associations.

3. Recognition of the rapidly growing need for public relations services in the international field and establishment of Hill and Knowlton international offices abroad, with representatives and associates throughout the world to serve both domestic and overseas clients.

4. Application of cost accounting and modern budget procedures in the practice of public relations.

5. Recognition of community relations as an important aspect of corporate and industrywide public relations with the development of techniques and personnel in this field.

6. Recognition of the growing interest of industry in giving financial and other cooperation to educational institutions, and the creation of a special department staffed by trained educators for the purpose of counseling clients in educational matters.

7. Creation of a professional-attitude research division in order to measure the dimension and quality of public relations problems.

Fortunately the public relations counseling business is unlike advertising in that among the top-grade firms the shifting of accounts from one firm to another is indeed a rarity. Moreover, the code of the Public Relations Society of America prohibits solicitation of a prospect that is already being served by another firm. The relations of public relations firms with their clients ordinarily is intimate and deeply immersed in policies and activities. It is a source of gratification that our new business has come from recommendations of clients as well as from good words spoken by our competitors in the counseling field.

I am often asked by young people about the opportunities for a career in public relations and how they should prepare for it. As for opportunities, the answer is much the same as it is in most other fields—the outlook is good for those who have the necessary qualifications. Public relations today is a lively, creative, fast-growing profession employing more than 40,000 people. I would predict that in ten years the number will be around 100,000. Several thousand companies, large and small, have their own public relations departments. There are more than 1,500 public relations agencies. In addition, public relations people are active in government, trade unions, church organizations, educational institutions, research groups and philanthropic and cultural campaigns.

More significant than growth in numbers is the fact that public relations has steadily increased in importance as a management function. This fact was emphasized by the findings of a 1962 survey carried out by the Program in Public Relations at Columbia University School of General Studies.

Of the 182 corporations responding to the survey questionnaire, 39 per cent said the person in charge of public relations is a member of the group that sets corporate policy. Seventy-seven per cent reported that the public relations head has access to management-policy discussions. Eighty-four per cent were of the opinion that the function of public relations is growing in importance.

I am sure that those are greatly higher percentages than would have been true no more than a decade ago. I think the trend to policy participation also was well expressed by the president of a large corporation who was quoted by the above-mentioned Program in Public Relations as stating:

> In the future I believe that the role of public relations will continue to grow. The increasing influence of public and governmental attitudes on the day-to-day conduct of our business requires that more emphasis be placed on evaluating these attitudes. We must be in a position to attune our business policies to the attitudes of the public or to explain our positions when we feel that these attitudes are harmful to our business and/or the national economy.

In the question of individual qualifications for this field, I have found that many young people are either ill-informed or very shallow in their thinking. My associates and I cannot number the times that young aspirants, describing their chief aptitude for public relations, have said something along these lines:

"I like people."

"I'm good at meeting people."

"I enjoy dealing with the public."

These of course are virtues that presumably should be helpful in almost any vocation. To the extent that they are valuable personality traits generally, they are helpful in public relations. But the "ability to get along with people" is not in itself a decisive grace. I have known successful public relations practitioners who were somewhat particular about whom they liked, and others who were something less than masterful at the ritual of meeting people. I have also seen gregarious back-slappers fail miserably when they faced up to the real tasks of their job.

The fact is, of course, that competence in public relations requires a combination of many qualities. I have mentioned integrity and judgment. I would also emphasize education and training. Four years of college have become virtually mandatory. Many men are now entering the field with master's degrees, and doctorates are not especially rare.

The college degree is important in getting a job, but more

telling are the dimensions of the learning the diploma represents. Courses in journalism and public relations are basically useful. But they are only a part of the background needed by the man or woman who would deal knowledgeably with business or other institutional problems in today's complex society. The preparation must be broader and deeper. It should emphasize history, economics, modern languages, philosophy, public affairs and other social sciences. Courses in law, business administration and corporate management are valuable.

I believe—as do most veterans of many years in public relations—that working in the editorial department of a newspaper provides excellent training. Some public relations firms and corporate departments will not hire a young man or woman unless the prospective employee has had several years' experience in newspaper work. The requirement is not necessarily for work on a large metropolitan daily, where the employee may be tied to one department. Experience on smaller papers where he does a variety of writing and editing can be excellent. The reason for this is not that press relations is all-important in public relations. Rather it is that in a newspaper office, objectivity, clarity and brevity are taught side by side with the human touch. So also are the abilities to work under pressure meeting deadlines, to gather information through interviews and source materials, to interpret facts and figures in understandable terms, and to exercise good judgment.

This is not to say that it is impossible to enter public relations through any other door. Many young people are succeeding in learning their skills on the job, either in the public relations department of a company or with a consulting firm. This manner of starting very probably will become more popular as corporate public relations departments grow and public relations firms become more numerous.

I suppose that just about every man who gives career advice warns that his particular field is full of hard knocks and hard work. I would be no exception. Frustrations are just as common in public relations as in most other endeavors, and I suspect more common than in many. Programs of action that seem important, fashioned with many days or months of intense work, are sometimes endlessly delayed or suddenly abandoned; teamwork is often at a premium; individual recognition may be difficult to come by; working hours, especially during emergencies, are long and often unpredictable.

There are assets, however, that can more than compensate. Good public relations people share in the excitement that comes from dealing with important problems and unexpected challenges. Their work often cuts across many departments of a corporation or an association, so that they participate in the broad phases of business action. There is frequently opportunity to do useful service for the community or society in general as a part of doing a good job. The field is still a fresh and buoyant one, largely unburdened by outmoded practices or prejudices. It is receptive to sound and progressive ideas. It is in the thick of the great currents of change and progress that are sweeping the world.

The matters public relations people deal with are almost as varied as the profuse facets of our daily lives. In business, they can involve taxation, stockholder activities, mergers, plant openings and plant closings, technological change, problems of health, labor relations, overseas relations, public understanding of needed or pending legislation, and introduction of new products—to name some.

The methods of communication of facts and ideas are also varied and numerous. Each of these areas and methods involves knowledge and techniques of its own; so there is a tendency among public relations people to specialize. The extent of specialization is likely to depend upon the size of the agency or department within a company.

My own organization necessarily employs a number of specialists—for example, in education, women's interests, press relations, radio and TV, art and graphics, promotion, and technical writing. Our account executives and management people must of course deal with divers problems across the board. But the specialists, also, usually need to keep themselves broadly informed. Their services often range over a wide cross section of client activities.

In stressing original educational requirements, I would by no means overlook the necessity for continuing self-education. The alert and knowledgeable public relations practitioner must keep up to date on the doings of business, government, science and other major fields through every means at his command. Obviously he must be an inveterate reader of newspapers, magazines, pertinent books, and analytical bulletins such as those put out by some of the leading banks. In our offices, among our own staff, the vital issues and developments of the hour are bound to come in for discussion virtually every day. Directly or indirectly, short range or long range, they bear on our work for our clients, and keeping abreast of them would be mandatory even if it were not an exciting part of living in the bargain.

Of course, this obligation to keep informed exists in all walks of life. Certainly it applies to businessmen, educators, public servants and clergymen, among many others. My point is simply that nowhere is it more indispensable than in public relations—and the man or woman who would enter the field without possessing this wide-ranging and lively interest is not likely to go far.

All that I have said of these attributes among staff members of a large organization applies equally to the small public relations firm or department.

I have no doubt about the continuing need for people who have the native qualities and acquired qualifications to make important contributions in the public relations field. There are and will be ample opportunities for those who are genuinely equipped and motivated to take advantage of them.

13

Public Opinion and Corporate Enterprise

WE hear so much about "the power of public opinion" in these times that we are apt to think of it as a political force of recent development. Everyone is aware that it was public opinion, expressed through hundreds of thousands of letters to members of Congress, that in 1962 defeated the Administration's tax withholding on personal income from dividends and interest. It was the pressure of public opinion that forced a reluctant Congress to place some restraints on labor by passing the Landrum-Griffin Act in 1959 and the earlier Taft-Hartley Act in 1947.

In the police state of Soviet Russia, it has been the tenacity of public opinion, in the form of defiance by Soviet youth, that has forced a disturbed government to accept critical native literature, to say nothing of western-style popular music and other alien enjoyments as a growing part of Ivan's cultural and social life.

But the fact is, of course, that public opinion has been recognized as the ultimate human force throughout history. Kings and rulers of antiquity courted it. Through the centuries, tyrants have feared ideas as much as swords and guns, for they have known that ideas catching hold of the minds of men can set into motion irresistible tides of public opinion.

Men seeking roles of leadership in free countries have made the support of public opinion their first goal knowing they cannot succeed without it.

No historic leader recognized the power of public opinion more astutely than did Lincoln, who observed: "In this age, and in this country, public sentiment is everything. With it, nothing can fail; against it, nothing can succeed. Whoever molds public sentiment goes deeper than he who enacts statutes or pronounces judicial decisions."

Public opinion—at least informed public opinion—exists on a far larger scale over the earth today than only a quarter of a century ago. Today education and communications are bringing literacy and knowledge where millions of people have lived in utter ignorance for centuries. This will not be changed in a year or a decade, but at least the start has been made—the great breakthrough has been achieved. Individuals in the remotest corners of the globe can read and hear about the vital events taking place in every other part of the earth. Now, with the Telstar, they will be able to see these events as well; the day of worldwide live television is at hand.

Because of this greatest revolution humanity ever has experienced—the revolution of scientific change—people throughout the world are becoming aware of how other people are living and what they are saying and doing.

Today we accept with casual interest a *New York Times* dispatch from Kenya, Africa, which reads:

> The sound of life in Kenya is not the cough of a lion, but that of the carpenter's hammer and the jet plane. Being built are a university, a television station, stores and a drive-in movie.

People everywhere have been fired with the contagious desire for better living and rising cultural standards. As opportunities multiply for the common man in free societies to become more fully aware of the world about him, over the years he will be increasingly in a position, if he chooses, to wield more influence on affairs than in any previous age.

Barbara Ward has said that "the citizen of today is not a voiceless, faceless man. He can influence government at every level."

In a word, the communications explosion has added greatly to the potential of public opinion, giving it new power and magnitude. However, it would be a grave error to speak of public opinion as a united, well-informed, easily understood voice of the people. It is united only on issues admitting no debate. For example, we can assume public opinion is for motherhood and against sin. But, when we look at debatable issues in politics, economics, religion and a thousand others, we hear a confusing chant of voices representing every conceivable shade and gradation of opinion, as well as of prejudice and emotional feeling.

That is why pollsters are kept busy in an effort to arrive at the best possible estimate of majority opinions or trends. In addition, there always are many straws flying in the wind for, in a free society, public opinion has no end of ways for expressing itself. It can make itself heard by word of mouth, in the press or, most effectively of all, at the polls and in the market place.

Obviously, public opinion cannot make government decisions. This power is delegated to elected officials. But public opinion can and does exert its influence ultimately and unmistakably upon their actions.

Public opinion falls into three main categories–misinformed, uninformed, and informed. The first two categories can be violently or passively destructive; the third almost invariably is a far more dependable and constructive influence.

No disaster short of a nuclear bomb could distress the Kremlin more than a collapse of the iron curtain and a flooding of Russia with information about the outer world. According to authoritative sources, Russia for a long period spent more each year to jam the Voice of America than we spend on the whole program the world over. In the 1963 thaw in the cold war, Russia ceased jamming the Voice at least temporarily.

The great forward strides of our times have brought problems as well as benefits insofar as the formation of public opinion is concerned. Our modern economic, political, and social issues have become so highly complicated that some historians are beginning to question whether a democracy can reach a rational consensus on them. The citizen today is bombarded incessantly from all sides with partisan arguments; he is urged to devote his attentions to a thousand immediate and pressing problems; he is expected to understand complex economic and even scientific issues, ranging from the country's gold position to the wisdom of allocating billions of dollars for a manned shot at the moon.

Because enlightened public opinion is the heart of a democracy, however, the solution is not to turn to a form of government in which the citizen's opinion would count for less. It is to inform him in ways that will help him to make his judgments count for more.

James Russell Lowell observed: "The foolish and the dead alone never change their opinion." Certainly we know that people's attitudes *do* change. We hope in this country that the logical presentation of facts will accomplish this and, of course, by informing public opinion, it often does. But it is oversimplification to suggest that facts alone can be expected to alter the basic views of everyone. Human attitudes, even among the most educated, tend to stem more from feelings and emotions than from cold logic. The mind of the college professor as well as the unschooled crop-picker is inclined to select and retain the facts it wants to retain—those facts that confirm established prejudices or leanings. How information is interpreted by the individual depends in part upon the racial, political or economic interests of the person, his background of culture and tradition, and his level of intelligence.

If you think this is a complex and baffling set of factors, of course you are right. It explains why, in a democracy, there are so many variations and shadings of opinion, so many conflicting pressure groups. Except in a few basic areas, let me repeat there is little unanimity of opinion on any basic subject or on any course of action.

Many organizations in America in carrying on public relations programs despair of broad appeals and direct their messages to so-called "opinion leader groups"—editors, writers, the clergy, educators, legislators, and other government leaders of all kinds. There are two reasons for this. One is the prohibitive cost of reaching 189 million people, and the other is the shoulder-shrugging indifference of great masses of people. They will give an ear to slogans and emotional appeals but shy away from any subjects outside their immediate experience. Curiosity and the awe of great office will attract people. But I have never felt that vast crowds about a President had much significance since I saw Herbert Hoover being mobbed by tens of thousands of people eager to see him while campaigning in Cleveland in October, 1932.

In public relations the hope is that the opinion leaders will get the message and, if convinced, serve as transmitters to their respective audiences. For example, a few editorials in the local newspapers in a congressional district will not only enlighten the people there, but will carry weight with the man from that district in Washington. But opinion leaders do not always "carry" the whole story to the people; so, large areas of public misunderstanding may remain. For some of the industries with which we have worked, public opinion polls show peaks of popular support and valleys of public indifference or of outright ignorance. Because of this, some industrial groups endeavor to go beyond the opinion leaders direct to the public, with fortnight, dramatic, and convincing appeals.

Those who would deal with public opinion must do so with all the understanding, intelligence and skill of which they are capable. Those of us who have spent may years in public relations know there are no easy short cuts to long-term public approval. We know that the approach to favorable public opinion in the case of a corporation, for example, begins with the *attitude* of top management toward its employees, shareholders, the people of its communities, its customers, and the general public interest.

Out of this attitude come policy decisions that determine the actions—the day-to-day performance—of the company as a whole. If public confidence is to be earned, these decisions must be made in the light of what is genuinely believed to be in the public interest. There can be no substitute for honest dealing with the people by any enterprise which wants to keep the respect of the public. Nor is there any magic or legerdemain in public relations that can convert a fake into a permanent value.

I have no patience with those who try to attribute insidious and mysterious powers to public relations. Such ideas are wholly fanciful and without basis in fact. Quacks, charlatans, and so-called "hidden persuaders" may come and go in the field of public relations but their time is short and their achievements ephemeral.

Nothing could be more absurd than to imagine that the so-called "corporate image" can be created by a clever use of words or by "slick" stunts. The ability of a specific business, or of business in general, to defend itself against its detractors and to project its worth to people begins with definitely existing policies and intrinsic values. The rightful purpose of public relations is openly to confirm, strengthen, and defend these values. Without integrity this cannot be accomplished.

It was not until the years of the Great Depression in the thirties that business in this country began to give much heed to the growth of public opinion as a dynamic social force. The New Deal was attacking business right and left with public approval, and it became more and more clear to enlightened managements that the very survival of our system of private enterprise was in danger. They realized then that their best ally would be an informed public opinion.

Out of this realization came a greatly accelerated effort by industry to earn and win the understanding and support of public opinion. It did this through policies and communications—the basic ingredients of public relations. As the problems of business have multiplied and broadened over the past thirty years, the scope and complexity of relationships with the public have grown tremendously in proportion.

Now let us leave no doubt in anyone's mind about the first responsibility of every business that wants to survive. It is to make a reasonable profit. But, rightly or wrongly, the public expects far more of today's corporation than the efficient operation of its business. It cannot consider itself a "private institution" in the sense that its policies and their impact are of concern only to its executives, stockholders, and employees. Whether it wishes or not, it is expected to go beyond the ability to prosper, and to be a community asset. It is viewed as a bearer of social responsibilities that are inseparable from its economic function. It must have its own definition of the national purpose, and it must have a concept of its own contribution to that purpose that it can publicly defend.

Business (or, for that matter, any major force in our society) can hope to win the support of public opinion only by speaking in a clear and positive voice. Merely to go to the wailing wall with complaints and criticisms rarely will win public sympathy. To do so is simply to give credence to suggestions such as that by President Kennedy that businessmen are obsessed with "a neurotic search for reassurance."

In America our dynamic capitalism has brought great prosperity and spread it among the people. Therefore, when industry speaks of the contributions of our system, its statements can be documented with facts familiar to all. Its own belief in the future of this system can affect the feelings and beliefs of all who have benefited from it. This does not mean that business can take the continued support of public opinion for granted—and very few businessmen indeed have any inclination to do so. But it does mean that, in speaking the truth, most of our corporations can point to deeds that prove this truth a reality. In speaking of the future, private enterprise can demonstrate that its objectives are fully attuned to the aspirations of the people.

We have observed that public opinion is fragmented, but this applies chiefly to controversial issues of current concern. Below the surface, like underground rivers, are deep-lying currents of opinion. These currents often are long hidden, and slow moving, but once tapped they are revealed as charged with great force.

It is not easy to sense these deeper currents of opinion, and often, to their sorrow, politicians as well as businessmen misread the signs.

Perhaps, if industry in the thirties had analyzed public opinion more carefully and had observed more closely the new standards rising in the public mind, it would have saved itself many a headache along with millions of dollars. Some of the big industries that bitterly fought union organization of their employees, in a fight foredoomed to failure, succumbed only at huge cost.

The leaders of this fight foresaw clearly the troubles now being forced upon us by big unions unrestrained by anti-trust laws and other legislation. But no power on earth could have halted the march of labor organization once it got under way. The voice of management, struggling for a principle that it believed to be in the national interest, was helpless in the face of this irresistible force backed by a deep current of supporting public opinion.

Seen in retrospect, it now is clear why many of the measures adopted by the New Deal—rightly or wrongly, for better or for worse—were destined to pass. They arrived not just because they had the solid backing of public opinion, but because public opinion had come to apply a new kind of standard in making its judgments about business performance.

The new measures were supported in the name of high moral issues, by slogans that made the most of "malefactors of great wealth," and of "human rights" as opposed to "property rights" exercised without conscience.

Standards and ideals of morality, of course, may vary widely, from nation to nation and from generation to generation. In some countries of the Middle East, for example, standards of honesty and fair dealing sometimes differ from our own; "Caveat Emptor" is considered a fair procedure. In this country, by contrast, our whole business and banking system is based on trust in others.

The standards of moral values and judgments of a country have their roots deep in the culture. And, although they are always subject to changes, the shifts usually come slowly.

In America, public standards of what is good and desirable have undergone profound changes since the turn of this century. There was a time when child labor, the twelve-hour day, and many other business practices, unacceptable today, were accepted by public opinion with but little criticism.

Many influences have been at work to change standards of opinion. University professors and other intellectuals have done their share. Then there was the slow awakening of the masses of people throughout the world, and the spreading of this spirit gradually everywhere. This spreading was fanned in America by social reformers seeking to improve the lot of the common man and by political reformers seeking the same end, with a bonus for themselves.

But perhaps the most potent of all the factors in changing the deep current of people's ideas have been the vast emotional and economic disturbances and upheavals resulting from two world wars.

Vast economic changes affecting the lives of all have occurred. The lot of most people in this country has been steadily improving as witnessed by rising standards of living. At the same time insecurity has spread as the majority of our people shifted over the years from self-employed to the state of employees on private and public payrolls. Most of these peope quite naturally think of income personally in terms of wages and salaries. They do not recognize the so-called "profit-motive" at work in themselves. Hence the management that explains its own motives *solely* in terms of profit-seeking speaks a tongue that to large numbers seems foreign, and needs extensive translation before it acquires warm meaning in terms of their own experience.

Management sometimes discovers that public opinion is insisting on moves that appear to be uneconomic. At such times it has the choice of yielding or taking a firm stand in opposition on principle. It is the privilege of every corporation, as of every citizen in America, to fight for what it believes is right and to attempt to persuade others to its view.

Moreover, the corporation has just as much right to expect fair and equitable treatment from the community as does any other decent, law-abiding citizen.

But it is not always safe to say to the community, "It is not *economic* to do what you want done," because the flood tide of public opinion is hard to resist.

The penalty for refusing the clear demands of public opinion may be management's loss of power or leadership. The new leadership, usually political, will see that public opinion gets what it wants. Management may be forced to accept certain standards that it had previously declared uneconomic —such as the eight-hour day, the minimum wage, and social security. Or it may be compelled to spend millions for such equipment as that for the prevention of air and stream pollution.

Sound policy, then, must pass the public-approval test, along with the profit-producing test, if a corporation is to feel itself secure on every front.

This is the bald fact headlined in all the economic legislation of the past quarter of a century.

And conversely, management needs to realize that not only will a policy that is unsound by public-interest standards fail because public opinion will force it to fail, but any effort to organize public opinion in behalf of unsound policy is also bound to fail.

Public relations can *organize* only that which, waiting for direction and focusing, exists already. Rarely, if ever—it may be emphasized—can public relations persuade any group, any society, to discard its deep-seated prevailing ideas of worth, of value, and of what is right and good.

When corporation policy *is* sound, it serves the community interest and is deserving of the support of public opinion. But this is not to say that it will get this support merely because it deserves it. The people must be informed. Lacking correct information they may withhold their support. This is a job for public relations.

With the best intentions in the world, managements intent on the immediate practical problems of profits, engineering, operations, expansion, sales, advertising, may sometimes overlook the equally practical problems of public relations in formulating policy decisions. When that happens it often proves to be a costly omission in our complex society.

To prevent possible errors of this kind, public relations officials are included in the policy-making group of an increasing number of leading corporations. Thus men whose minds are attuned to problems of public relations which may be involved in policy decisions are present at the discussion stage.

Public relations counsel with a wide range of experience and an objective outside viewpoint also are frequently consulted on various phases of policy matters. More and more members of top management of the new generation understand the policy-level significance of public relations.

In making its decisions and trying to forecast their outcome, management must keep a constant eye on the shifting regulations of government commissions; on laws constantly rewritten to please special groups; on the tactics of a union monopoly that seeks always fresh ways to apply duress; on the pressure of ever-increasing competition for markets; on the requirement that stockholders be somehow kept satisfied, among all the others, if management is to attract the capital needed for corporate growth.

A challenge can arise at almost any time out of any of these groups, to confront management with demands that it justify its performance, or its use of authority, or the objectives it seeks, or its own value to the American community—in terms of the policies it follows and the decisions it makes.

Every such challenge, however it relates to performance, also concerns policy—and is a public relations problem. One can hardly repeat too often that public relations begins with policy, rises out of policy, dramatizes policy, explains policy, and constantly reaffirms the value of sound policy.

14

"What's in It for Me?"

AS I look back on thirty-six years of practice in the field of public relations, I am forced to wonder why seemingly so little progress has been made in the economic education of Americans.

Secretary of Commerce Luther Hodges has asked how the United States can expect to grow and prosper if so many "of our people, to put it bluntly, are economic boobs."

Possibly the word "boob" may be too harsh. But certainly we have to reach the conclusion that a great lack of understanding exists when Dr. George Gallup, after a quarter century of opinion polling, is led to make this observation:

"Apparently college students have never had to distinguish between federal and local spending—and when we ask college graduates to cite the advantages of our economic system over that of the Russians, half of them cannot name even one advantage . . ."

Opinion Research Corporation has conducted surveys of high-ranking high school graduates that show that many believe standards of living can be improved simply by raising wages or increasing government spending. Barely one in four understands that the basic way to raise the standard of living is to produce more goods per man-hour.

According to this same survey organization, there has been an inching trend year by year toward popular belief that government should control the profits of large corporations. Last year the researchers found that 43 per cent of the public held this belief. Here is a breakdown of categories of people who, according to Opinion Research Corporation, favored government control over profits—25 per cent of the public:

18 per cent of those of above average income.
18 per cent of stockholders.
13 per cent of professional men and 20 per cent of managers.
23 per cent of white collar workers.
25 per cent of farmers.
30 per cent of unskilled workers.
22 per cent of union members.

In another study, it was found that, among the fallacies regarded as facts by many Americans, are these:

1. Profits result from exploitation.
2. The profit system is a wicked institution designed to grind down the poor.
3. Profit-making is a system of greed and avarice.
4. Profit-makers are expropriators of money earned by workers.
5. Thus, there should be strict government regulation and strict confiscatory taxation.

These are unpleasant and unpalatable facts for businessmen, but they are juicy morsels for many politicians who fatten on them. Of the 75,000 to 100,000 bills introduced each year in our state legislatures, a large proportion is aimed at increased regulation over business. I do not mean to imply that these measures are all bad or harmful. But many of them are proposed by people who are unsympathetic to business or at least find it politically expedient to be so. And we cannot overlook the fact that legislative acts hostile to business usually have the support of public opinion.

In the first session of the 1962 Congress, four of five of the major bills considered involved new regulations on business or more requirements for costly business reporting and other red-tape procedures. Many of these bills were aggressively proposed and pushed by the Executive Branch of the government.

For private enterprise, these facts represent a grim and far-reaching public relations problem. The remarkable resiliency of private enterprise, its dynamic drive, and its incomparable ability to adjust to changing conditions in providing products, services, and jobs for people—all this will survive only as long as the profit motive is permitted to function.

In the first dozen years after 1950, private enterprise suffered a seriously declining profit rate. Profits, after taxes, for manufacturing corporations, as a per cent of net worth, fell 41 per cent. In the same period, the average hourly earnings excluding overtime of production workers in manufacturing, including benefits, went up 62 per cent. At the same time, government acts and measures encroached steadily upon managements' powers of decision on vital matters affecting profits, such as wages and prices.

While there is every indication that government intervention in the economy is now taken for granted by most people, the question of what kind of intervention and how far it is to go has not been resolved.

So the problem is, how far is this kind of encroachment to be carried? What is the proper separation of government and management responsibilities? I already have made the point, and repeat it here, that the power of decision on vital matters such as wages and prices carries with it the responsibility for the successful operation of a business. You cannot separate decision from responsibility.

It is not too much to say that private enterprise stands at the crossroads; and in the answers to these questions lies the direction in which it will go. At stake is the fate of the private enterprise system and of the social institutions that have built America. Government as an impartial referee is one thing, but government as a policeman using a loaded club on business is quite another. If the future is to hold continuing encroachments by government, socialism will be the inevitable outcome. If that is what the majority of people want, they will get it. Right now the public is inclined, without realizing where they are headed, to support piecemeal many of the separate bits and parts of legislation which, when put together, add up to socialism. How such a change may come about in this country was described in an article first published in the spring of 1947 in a magazine, *The Partisan Review*, and reprinted in the *Congressional Record* of September 26, 1961. The article was entitled "The Future of Socialism—The Perspective Now." It says in part:

> If socialism (i.e., the ownership by the state of all significant means of production) is to preserve democracy it must be brought about step by step in a way which will not disrupt the fabric of custom, law, and mutual confidence upon which personal rights depend. That is, the transition must be piecemeal; it must be parliamentary; it must respect civil liberties and due process of law. Socialism by such means used to seem fantastic to the hard-eyed melodramatists of the Leninist persuasion; but even Stalin is reported to have told Harold Laski recently that it might be possible.
>
> There seems no inherent obstacle to the gradual advance of socialism in the United States through a series of New Deals. In 1933, Frances Perkins has reported, the coal operators pleaded with the government to nationalize the mines.

> They offered to sell "to the government at any price fixed by the government. Anything so we can get out of it." The government was not ready to take over the coal mines in 1933, as it was not ready to take over the banks, as it was not ready to keep the railroads in 1919. But the New Deal greatly enlarged the reserves of trained personnel; the mobilization of industry during the war provided more experience; and the next depression will certainly mean a vast expansion in government ownership and control. The private owners will not only acquiesce in this. In characteristic capitalist panic, they will demand it.

When this article was reprinted in the *Congressional Record*, it attracted wide comment because its author was Arthur M. Schlesinger, Jr., who had been a professor of history at Harvard University when he wrote it and in 1961 was one of President Kennedy's influential advisers. In a letter to Senator Hugh Scott under date of June 2, 1962, Mr. Schlesinger vigorously denied that he was a socialist or that the article reflected his views. He wrote:

"I was asked, as a scholar, to contribute to a symposium on 'The Future of Socialism' and did so, but as an analyst, *not* as an advocate. The fact that I, as an historian, participated in a symposium on the future of socialism no more makes me a socialist than participation in a symposium on 'The Future of the Steel Industry' would make me Roger Blough."

Even though Mr. Schlesinger himself is not a socialist, opinion polls would seem to indicate that the revolution in the economic order as described by him would be acceptable to an uncomfortably large segment of the people of the United States. Today this is a minority segment but, year by year, it has been growing.

What are the causes of public indifference or antipathy toward business? They lie, I believe, in two main areas:

1. *The remoteness of big business.* In order to provide for the needs of a large population in a vast country, big business like big government is indispensable. This fact seems to be widely accepted by the people. But the bigger the business has become, the more remote it has grown from the people whom it serves. This is an unavoidable paradox. Its vast operations, its giant facilities, its multimillion-dollar finances are simply beyond the experience of the average man. To him, big business, though recognized as necessary, is unfamiliar and, accordingly, misunderstood in many of its aspects.

2. *Widespread economic illiteracy.* The late Burton Crane said that "the American economy is the eighth wonder of the world. The ninth is the economic ignorance of the American people." The most disturbing element of this ignorance is the woeful lack of understanding of the vital role of profits in the economy. As we have seen, surveys of public opinion have shown a prevalence of the bizarre idea that profits are the "gravy" for a rapacious few. The need for profits to provide or to attract the capital necessary to modernize and expand plants and make more jobs seems to be lost on large segments of the public. This is the heart of industry's problem.

Out of these misconceptions have grown widely accepted economic myths that play directly into the hands of political opportunists and doctrinaire leftists. Among the most common of such myths are these:

1. Corporate profits go into the pockets of the managers of business.

The fact is, of course, that management people are salaried employees, retained by the owners—the stockholders. Nor do the owners get all the profits by any means. A large part must go into improvement and growth of the business.

2. The great bulk of the money a company gets from its sales is kept as profits.

The money that companies are managing to keep as profits is a small percentage of the sales dollar, and is still shrinking. On the average for manufacturing companies, in 1961, profits after taxes were 4 cents out of every dollar. This is the most serious problem in our economy.

3. Wages can be increased indefinitely without raising prices. If necessary, wage raises can be taken out of profits.

Largely because it is so aggressively promoted by labor leaders, this myth is the most widespread. At the same time, it is probably the most damaging to the nation's economic future. Wage increases that devour earnings and cannot be met through price increases or adequate cost reductions because of competitive pressure leave the company little or nothing on which to grow. In the end, enterprises thus affected either cannot compete or have not the means to invest in new efficiencies and products, in either of which case their ability to provide jobs goes down.

4. Prices can be raised without regard to competition.

This fallacy probably had its origin in the years of shortages immediately following World War II. No idea could be in greater error now. Not only must competition with other U.S. producers be considered, but we have entered into a new era of international competition in which trade barriers are coming down and goods are flowing ever more freely across world borders. More and more, American goods must compete directly with products made in low-wage countries and sent into our own U.S. markets as well as throughout the world.

5. Stocks in the nation's corporations are held by only a few rich people.

This myth is beginning to abate somewhat since millions of wage earners are themselves stockholders in business. Nevertheless, the notion still is prevalent that corporations are operated for the benefit of a greedy few, and the fact that corporate stocks are owned by 17 million Americans in all walks of life still is relatively unappreciated.

6. Government control of business has nothing to do with freedom of the individual.

We constantly encounter people, young and old, who see nothing wrong in ever-increasing government control of business and assume that there is no threat to the individual liberties they have come to take for granted. The truth is, of course, that every increase in government control brings a decrease in freedom of the individual citizen.

It is an oversimplification to suggest that economic myths exist only among the general populace or groups who, through indifference or otherwise, have not availed themselves of the facts. Our economic efforts are saddled by myths persisting even in high places, not the least of which may be found within the government itself. Consider these views which have been strongly advocated in Washington at one time or another over the past thirty years.

1. The government can impose discriminatory taxes on American enterprise abroad without harming the ability of American business to compete with big and aggressive foreign companies in the international markets.

2. If the environment for growth in private capital spending is made unfavorable, large increases in federal spending can make up for it.

3. Consumers generally tend to buy things they do not need or want because they succumb to advertising and marketing pressures; therefore, government regulators should supervise the consumers' freedom of choice by controlling the advertising and marketing activities of industry.

4. The only achievements capable of "moving the economy forward" are those of the Federal government; and

whether the nation is successfully meeting its problems is measured, not by the advancements and freedoms of its people, but by the growth in the Federal budget and the number of bureaucrats on the job.

What can be done to raise the level and quality of economic understanding by the public? This is a question increasingly asked but with no easy answer. Certainly the times call urgently for new approaches, new forms of action.

If there is to be real education, it must come from all the sources capable of providing it. First, of course, there are the nation's schools. Many anxious citizens have urged that greater emphasis be placed on the realistic economics of the private enterprise system in our schoolrooms from the elementary grades through the highest degrees at the university level.

Owners, publishers, and editors of the nation's great communications media—newspapers, magazines, television and radio—can play a vital part in broadening economic education and making it more attractive. Many already are doing this. Large service institutions, such as many of the foundations, could provide no greater service to the nation than to initiate or enlarge their activities in this field. Certainly the officials of government have an obligation to help develop a better understanding among the people. Many of our representatives in government—particularly the well-known champions of the private-enterprise system in Congress—are doing yeoman service.

Above all, I believe major responsibilities rest with American business—with those who must assume leadership in the defense and growth of the enterprise system.

What are these responsibilities? Here are some of them, in terms of public relations goals to which business must give its best attention:

1. The number one public relations job of business is to

establish its identity with the people. Business in a free economy is the means by which the people create wealth, jobs, and a rising standard of living. It serves the people and is essential to their lives and well-being. Let all business come to a dead halt for one month and the nation would suffer an indescribable calamity.

2. In undertaking to inform and enlighten public opinion, industry must learn to communicate with people in terms they understand and believe. It is not enough to be believable only, it is important also to be interesting. Business has acquired a jargon of its own, largely based on the terminology of the accountants, and this jargon simply does not get through to the man on the street. Surveys have shown that words like "surplus," "depreciation," and "net income" leave the average person floundering in confusion. Business, it is clear, has been largely talking to itself for years. It needs to use language that all can understand.

3. The average person is not a trained economist. He does not view an industry issue or problem with academic objectivity. Rather he is inclined to say to himself regarding this or that issue: "How does it affect me?" or "What's in it for me?" Let industry people ponder these perfectly natural and human questions and learn how to answer them. No idea could be more absurdly futile than that it is possible to turn 189 million people into objective economists.

In order to talk to the people and ask them to understand *industry's* problems, it is important to understand people and *their* problems. Whatever happens to the economy does in fact affect the average man. The problem is to bridge the gap in his understanding between the economic facts of life and his own personal pocketbook.

The truth is that most people live in little worlds of their own. The interest of each individual is centered chiefly in his home, his family, his job, his group, his union, and his neighborhood. He thinks in terms of his world, and affairs beyond it seem abstract and remote and get little serious consideration. Yet, in our complex society, this is a dream world, wholly unrealistic. No one in these times can live untouched by outside events.

Unemployment or the need to change employment may come to large numbers from causes over which they have absolutely no control. The vast migration from rural to urban life is not a matter, in the large, of individual decision. Mechanization of the farms has freed millions of people from the necessity of earning a living from the soil. They have drifted to towns, cities, and factory centers.

The decline of the textile industry in New England, changing modes of transportation, and foreign competition are just a few of the many forces that have affected the lives of people. In steel alone, the influx of certain products from abroad in recent years has taken the jobs of 52,000 workers. Automation, of course, has swept through many industries as each has desperately sought ways to maintain profits in the face of maddeningly rising costs.

All of these factors have caused an enormous social and economic impact upon modern life. Many individuals who had lived contentedly in their little world have been shaken out of it into a state of frustration and helplessness. To them it is understandable why the ministrations of the welfare state should be welcome.

The fact is that the staggering spending programs by government at all levels have public approval and, in good measure, are in response to public demand for services or handouts. The tragic irony of this is that people forget the only source of government money is from their own pockets through inflation or taxes, or both.

4. Businessmen cannot deal with these perfectly natural and human feelings by ignoring them. They must develop a

keener sensitivity to public attitudes. This has come to be a requirement of as great importance for modern business management as it is for political leaders. In a sense, management men in private enterprise are political officeholders responsible not only to shareholders, employees, customers, and communities but to public opinion as well. For this reason, it behooves them to keep the public fully informed on matters of public concern. They also must be equipped and able in the arena of public affairs. The host of government bureaus, regulations, laws, and administrators bearing upon business makes competence in dealing with officialdom an indispensable qualification for today's managements.

5. Where hostility in public opinion exists, its roots should be uncovered and steps taken to correct it. If policies are unsound or out of step with the identifiable public interest, they should be studied and, if possible, corrected. Quite often the remedy called for is more information to the public together with forthright explanation and interpretation.

6. One of the most acute of all problems confronting industry today is the tremendous political and economic power of the giant labor unions. Business has many legal restraints; the unions have virtually none. They have a monopoly power that can strangle the economy at will. All this has happened with the full permission of public opinion. But if public opinion comes to realize that too much union power can be as harmful to the national interest as too much financial power, reasonable restraints upon unions as well as upon business may become the order of the day. Everyone will suffer if industry gets into trouble because of union-imposed overburdensome costs. And many feel that we already have reached that perilous point through the combined pressures of politically aligned big labor and big government.

7. One thing above all is certain: the cause of private

enterprise can be defended successfully only if business is willing to fight. Businessmen are being urged on all sides to enter more vigorously into political activity. Many have continued to hold back, fearing that they would alienate customers. But the proponents of more attention to politics have pointed out that, as one Dallas newspaper editor has put it, the alternative may be to wake up some morning and find that they have "no business, let alone any customers, to worry about losing."

Of even greater concern is the fact that we apparently have reached the point in this country where businessmen must face up to possible deliberate government coercion and intimidation. During the 1962 congressional session, our firm was working with an organization of a large number of American companies who were opposing what they considered an unfair tax measure. The measure had passed the House in the previous session and then went before a Senate committee. We were told that some of the heads of companies who had been most effective in testifying before the House Committee would not participate in the Senate hearings. The reason given: their companies, in the interim, had been singled out for unusual harassment by government agencies and there were hints of more to come. Because of the threat of such harassment, we were told, there were other businessmen who also shied away from presenting their case at the Senate hearings even though their companies had mucl at stake.

During this same period, a business writer for one of the nation's major newspapers asked a group of businessmen how the proposed measure would affect their companies' operations. The writer, who was himself neutral on the issue, said: "I am having trouble getting quotes for attribution. Many of the heads of companies whom I call tell me why the bill would be bad for the economy but they ask not to be quoted by name. They are afraid of reprisals from Washington. To me, it is a very disturbing sign."

I do not want to give the impression that this was a general business attitude. Many businessmen went to Washington and spoke up forcefully and vigorously in opposition to the bill. Neither do I want to imply that the Administration has been using illegal pressures in these instances. In fact, some businessmen are convinced that a more sympathetic attitude toward business has developed in Washington. They cite various policies such as tax reduction, more liberal depreciation, and President Kennedy's favorable reaction to the 1963 steel price advances, as evidence of a better climate.

Obviously the Administration was unhappy with the anti-business stigma placed upon it and would like to see it removed. This is all to the good. It gives encouragement to business in its efforts to achieve better understanding, but it gives no cause for complacency. Efforts should not be lessened, but rather increased, for only by keeping public opinion constantly informed and alert can business hope to win the support either of the people or government.

The problem for business is to find ways to talk to people in terms of their own interests and to bring realism into their dream worlds. The irresistible tide of events is likely to play a controlling part in this undertaking. Although the average man may be loath to look beyond his own doorstep—beyond his own little local circle—he can hardly fail to note, as time goes on, the compelling effect of outside influences upon his life and fortune.

Such questions as foreign competition, inflation, government deficits, the role of profits and of labor costs are not remote academic abstractions but hard realities of everyone's daily life. Recognition of these facts by public opinion will not come easily; but unless it does come, there can be no approach to economic sanity in this country.

Public opinion may be informed and enlightened in many ways. The so-called "opinion leaders"—the politicians, editors, writers, clergy, educators, and articulate people in numerous categories—play an essential role in the formation of public opinion. It is important that these leaders have correct information soundly presented that they can, if they will, pass on to the millions of people whose attitudes they influence. If their ideas are unsound, their influence is negative or worse. Every well-organized public relations program should give great attention to the job of providing adequate information to opinion leaders. When they do not pass on the story to the people, as I have pointed out in another chapter, it then becomes necessary to go direct to the people.

These are some of the reflections that occur to me as I look back and wonder at the continuing widespread economic illiteracy in the face of all the years of effort by business groups to generate a better understanding of the economic facts of life. My conclusion is that public "education" is an endless job and at best it will never make us a nation of disciplined economists. The appeal must be more to the emotions than to the intellect, and it must be directed to the individual's self-interest.

Public opinion has enormous power when aroused, but it also has a vast indifference to the problems of industry and an abysmal unawareness of economics.

The educational job to be done is great and continuing. It is necessary to teach the alphabet to each new generation. Every child must learn anew the lessons its parents once learned. But it is useless for business to expect that the common man is going to become interested in its problems, its profit position, or its balance sheet until he can be shown how all this affects him, his life, his job, and his well-being.

So the work of economic education, of improving public understanding of the private enterprise system, must go on and on. It is a fearsome challenge but not an insuperable one. As long as there are millions of Americans determined to fight *for* the freedoms of democracy and *against* the regimentation of socialism, we have good reason to hope that it will be met.

15

International Public Relations

IT has been said that four main revolutions are occurring in the world today:

> The rising expectations of underdeveloped peoples.
>
> The economic development in non-Western countries—the effort to achieve five centuries of change in a few decades.
>
> The scientific advance, with emphasis on the revolution in weaponry, space, communications, and transportation.
>
> The achievement of the European Common Market and the rise of a third great world power.

This latter development is certain to have a profound impact both upon the markets of the world and international political affairs. This is true whether or not in the end Great Britain is permitted to come into the fold.

It is a noteworthy but obscure fact of history that an American, John J. McCloy, helped to generate and develop the idea that was later to become the Common Market. The account in the following three paragraphs has been authorized by Mr. McCloy.

Mr. McCloy, who served as High Commissioner for Germany from 1949 to 1952, spent a weekend in 1949 with Robert Schuman, former Prime Minister of France, then French Minister of Foreign Affairs. In their far-ranging talks about the future of Europe the revolutionary concept of pooling the coal and iron resources of the Continent was evolved. During the same period, McCloy was talking with his old friend, Jean Monnet, with whom he had been associated first while Monnet was a partner in the New York banking firm of Blair & Co., for which firm McCloy had performed legal services.

McCloy had also been close to Monnet during the period the latter had been an important factor in the Allied Purchasing Commission and McCloy had been the Assistant Secretary of War. Discussions, which resulted in the Schuman Plan, continued with Monnet playing an ever-increasing role while McCloy was able to guide thought in Germany through his position as American High Commissioner.

Incidentally, McCloy was detailed to sound out the British as to their attitude toward the union of European and British interests as Schuman was convinced that nothing could come of the full plan unless Britain was a participant. Thus it would have been possible for Britain to write its own ticket of entry but McCloy met with a very cold reception both in Whitehall and the city. On March 9, 1951, six nations joined together to draft a treaty putting the Schuman plan into effect. By now everyone was aware that behind the progress of the plan was the boundless enthusiasm and drive of Jean Monnet.

In June, 1952, all six nations—France, Italy, The Netherlands, West Germany, Belgium and Luxembourg—had ratified the treaty and the European Coal and Steel Community was in being. Another American, George W. Ball, then an international lawyer, now Undersecretary of State, had taken an active part in the work leading to the adoption of the Community. As legal aid to Jean Monnet, he had drafted the charter.

Jean Monnet was jubilant over the advent of the Community because he saw in it a first tangible move toward the realization of his dream of a political union in Europe. His unswerving perseverance toward that goal has made him one of the great leaders of our time. He and his adherents provide living proof of the irresistible power of a sound idea, communicated with intelligence, enthusiasm, and persistence.

Because of my interest in the international field, I had a great desire to meet Jean Monnet. On a trip to Europe in 1955, I carried a letter of introduction to him from my friend, Chester McLain, a long-time partner and associate of Mr. McCloy. I did not meet Monnet in Europe but the opportunity came on the return trip on the *Queen Mary*.

He was in a relaxed mood but when I asked him about the Coal and Steel Community he spoke of it eloquently and with intense feeling. "This is only the first step in a grand design," he said. "The second step will be the Common Market. And the third step will be a political unity—a United States of Europe. That is the ultimate goal.

"Most people do not realize how near we are to political unity in Europe. They simply will not believe it. But it is close, very close. The Common Market will come and this will bring into being a great unified trading area rivaling yours in the United States. The full maturity of the Common Market will mean free movement of people and goods within an area having a population (if Great Britain and other European countries join) of 258,762,000."

I saw Mr. Monnet again a few days later in New York at a small dinner given for him at the Union Club by Clarence

Randall. At this dinner he repeated the views he had expressed to me on the liner. George Ball was also a guest at the Randall dinner and Mr. Monnet asked him to talk with me at further length next day. Accordingly, Mr. Ball came to my apartment the following afternoon and we had a long discussion on international public relations, a subject in which he had a keen interest.

The views of Mr. Monnet and Mr. Ball on the way events were taking shape in Europe confirmed my own faith in the economic future of the continent, and encouraged me to persist in the effort to build a public relations service in Europe. In succeeding years there was every indication that Mr. Monnet's grand concept was gaining acceptance. But when Charles de Gaulle came into power and his views became known, it was seen they were not in harmony with those of Mr. Monnet. De Gaulle obviously wants a federation of European fatherlands led by France, not an integrated United States of Europe. The issue remains to be resolved in the years ahead but the Monnet concept suffered a serious setback when de Gaulle early in 1963—without consulting his five Common Market partners—vetoed Great Britain's entry into an expanded community.

In May of 1963, *The New York Times* reported that Mr. Monnet had somewhat altered his views as a result of the exclusion of Britain from the EEC. He was said to have concluded that European political union now must derive directly from a pro-European defense and foreign policy (including Britain), rather than arise in the process of achieving economic unity.

Despite these hitches in the Common Market development, I have not changed my view of the long-range outlook for Europe that I have held since 1952. In that year traveling from country to country in postwar Europe I became conscious of a powerful renewal of the movement toward higher standards of living that World War II had interrupted. It seemed to me that the change that was taking place from a bicycle to an automobile economy symbolized what was happening in every aspect of the European scene. Between 1948 and 1960, the registration of motor cars there increased more than 250 per cent compared with 77 per cent in the U.S.

In London in 1952, I met a young public relations man, Alan Campbell-Johnson, who, within a few years of practice, already had gone to the top of his field in Great Britain. He had served as press attaché to Lord Mountbatten during the Transfer of Power in India. He is the author of a number of books including *Mission with Mountbatten* and biographies of Anthony Eden and Lord Halifax. Lady Tweedsmuir, who has been a Conservative Member of Parliament since 1946, was for ten years until her appointment as a Minister in the Macmillan Government a co-director of his firm.

Campbell-Johnson and I had many meetings, and formed what was to be a close and long-lasting association of our firms. We agreed that the time rapidly was approaching when Europe's economy would blossom and with this would come a growing need for public relations services. We decided on a plan for a network of associated firms in European countries and I was to proceed in making the arrangements. I realized that this was a long-term project and Campbell-Johnson and I agreed that it might take us ten years before our plans could come to fruition. It seemed necessary to me to first align ourselves with experienced practitioners in the various European countries, rather than establish branches of our American operation in these places.

In Paris I met Eric Cypres, representative of the *New York Herald Tribune*, an able Belgian with energy and enthusiasm. He was eager to open an office in Brussels. In The Hague was Frans Hollander, former head of the Planning Department of the Information Service of The Netherlands Government, and Director of Information for the Royal Netherlands Army. In Paris was Frank Bauer, well-known publicist and a pioneer in the public relations counseling field in France.

These men formed the nucleus of Europe's first public relations network. For ten years we have worked together closely as a team that subsequently has been enlarged by professionals from other European nations.

Shortly after my return to New York, I had a visit from a young Dutchman named Loet Velmans, then living in New York. He said he had heard from friends in Paris about my plans and he was applying for a job in our new international division. I wondered where he got this accurate information so speedily and later learned it had come from a partner of George Ball in their Paris law office. Among the qualifications Velmans advanced in his favor was the fact that he was multilingual. I was impressed but had not expected to hire anyone immediately, so I thought to discourage him by saying that anyone hired then in our embryo international division would have to come in at a most modest salary. He said, "I am not looking for a big salary, I am looking for a big opportunity." He got the job. Velmans worked in our New York headquarters for three years; then I sent him to Europe. Today as president of Hill and Knowlton International at Geneva, Switzerland, he directs and coordinates all of our European operations.

One day at lunch in 1954 I discussed with the president of a large international oil-company client some of his company's problems in many parts of the world. It was agreed that our firm would send a two-man team around the world to study the company's public relations problems and to organize a program. I picked Velmans as a member of the team. Merrick Jackson, a vice president of Hill and Knowlton, Inc., who had just been married when I handed him this assignment, had to choose between an around-the-world trip and his honeymoon. He postponed the honeymoon. The program developed as a result of that survey still serves as the blueprint for the company's worldwide public relations activities.

About this time we made another excursion into the international field. An oil-company client drilling in western Australia had struck oil. Because the oil had the consistency of axle grease there would be some delay in determining its commercial value. Until more was known, it was decided that a policy of strict secrecy would be observed.

Unfortunately, there was a leak. Pandemonium broke loose on the Australian stock exchange. Oil shares skyrocketed beyond all reason and, to complicate matters, there was an outburst of criticism against the oil company for having held back the "good" news. Company officials were falsely accused of speculating in the shares. All this had serious implications for the company that shortly would be seeking to renew its leases.

Because the company had no public relations facilities in Australia, we were asked to fly someone to the scene at once. Richard W. Darrow, now executive vice president of our firm, was given the assignment. Darrow gathered the facts and presented them to newspaper editors and other important opinion leaders in key centers. The result was a gradual return to sanity on the part of the press and the public. But it became obvious that there was continuing work to be done. At the oil company's urgent request, we set up a Hill and Knowlton subsidiary in Australia that continued to operate as long as its services were needed. The controlling interest in the subsidiary was then sold to Eric White, a large operator in Australia. As for oil in western Australia, all indications known to geological science seemed to assure the existence of a big field in the area of the first well. But, unaccountably, nature tricked the geologists. Many other drillings and many millions of dollars later, the company had nothing to show but a dismal series of dry holes.

In 1954, our international horizon was broadened further by two events. The first was our acquisition of the Edward W. Barrett organization. In taking over this firm, we not only added the able former Assistant Secretary of State to our executive staff, but we acquired a number of international accounts—notably the Government of Japan and the Suez Canal Company.

The unpredictability of events in today's world of violence and upheaval never was more dramatically revealed than in the case of the Suez Canal. Early in 1956, I attended a small dinner at the Century Club in New York at which the guest of honor was Jacques Georges-Picot of Paris, president of the Suez Canal Company. Mr. Georges-Picot explained that the company's contract with Egypt provided for turning over control of the Canal to that country in 1968. I asked him if there was any danger of seizure prior to that time.

"No, not the slightest," replied Mr. Picot with emphasis. "We have every assurance on that score."

A few months later on July 26, 1956 Nasser seized the Canal and on October 29, 1956, England, France, and Israel began their ill-fated intervention. About a year later we resigned the account voluntarily. Suez Canal Company had transformed itself into a holding and investment concern, and for the time being at least there was no specific work we could do on its behalf in the U.S.

Ed Barrett remained with our firm until 1956 when he resigned to become Dean of the Graduate School of Journalism at Columbia University.

The second significant event in the firm's international business in 1954 was its appointment as American public relations counsel for the Brussels World's Fair, 1958. This account, obtained through the good offices of Eric Cypres in Brussels, was the first important breakthrough by our European network. It brought us into an entirely new field and introduced me to a remarkable man, Count Moens de Fernig, High Commissioner of the World's Fair for the Belgian Government. He is a gentleman of great charm, boundless energy and consummate administrative skill. The outstanding success of the Fair was due to his drive and direction.

Our work in America for the Fair pleased the Count and he subsequently appointed our network to handle public relations problems in many countries on the continent and in Great Britain. The success of the effort to bring the Fair to the attention of the U.S. public is measurable by the fact that the number of Americans traveling to the Benelux countries rose from 175,000 in the previous year, or 31 per cent of all American visitors in Europe, to 290,000, or 46 per cent of American visitors in 1958.

The World's Fair program gave our European associates their first major test of working together as a team. Cypres and Velmans coordinated the program that contributed to the attraction of more than 40 million visitors during 1958. On the day of the press preview, a record attendance of some fifteen hundred journalists was reported. Assisting the World's Fair internal public relations staff, about ten executives from the United States and our associates in Europe dealt with the multitude of reporters.

During the Fair, the High Commissioner lived in the impressive Belvedere Palace nearby. The palace had two dining rooms and every weekday he had forty guests for lunch, with eighteen in one dining room where he was host and twenty-two in the other where his wife, the Countess Moens de Fernig, presided. On the day I was there, Adlai Stevenson and his two sons also were guests as were Howard Cullman, United States Commissioner at the Fair, and Mrs. Cullman. The Count introduced me to Mr. Stevenson and we were chatting for a moment when inevitably the subject of politics arose. I said, "I must confess, Mr. Stevenson, that I am a Republican—a dyed-in-the-wool Taft man." "Well," he replied, with a smile, "that is not a capital offense—yet."

From 1952 on, the signs were increasingly clear that Europe was hurrying into a boom. This materialized and has since leveled out somewhat, but the gigantic potentialities of the Common Market remain to be realized.

Over the years I became more and more determined to strengthen and broaden our European facilities. Thus, when the Common Market arrived, we were prepared.

Numerous American companies are alive to this development and are going to Europe for the first time or, if they are already there, are expanding activities. The demand for our services comes largely from such companies.

The Common Market is bringing many problems of establishing company and product identification over a wide area; of building goodwill in a vast market; of recruiting competent young executives; of providing information to employees, stockholders, customers, and the public.

Our service to clients in Europe is on the same order as that made available by our parent firm in America. We provide counsel to management on public relations problems; we make public relations surveys and develop plans and programs; we advise on stockholder and employee communications; and we handle relations with the press and, in various countries, relations with government officials, as well.

Fortunately, many corporations are now convinced that the task of public relations abroad should not be confined to the dissemination of product releases. United States companies that have a large stake in the protection of their corporate reputation at home cannot run the risk of seeing this same reputation deteriorate abroad.

Our problem, as we saw it, was to combine the talents of professionals experienced in American public relations practice with those of topnotch European practitioners intimately acquainted with conditions in their own countries.

Further, as European unity becomes more and more a reality, the need for close coordination of programs in various countries increases. To meet this need we took another step in Geneva, expanding the staff with the addition of several men who had U.S. public relations experience and were also thoroughly familiar with the region assigned to them.

As president of our European headquarters company, Hill and Knowlton, S.A., of Geneva, Velmans carries overall responsibility for coordinating operations in all European countries. An important part of management is an executive committee, of which Alan Campbell-Johnson of England and Eric Cypres of Belgium are members together with officials of the parent company in New York. This committee plays an active role in planning and reviewing client programs. Our team of specialists at Geneva headquarters works closely with our associates in each country to provide a unified approach to a wide variety of public relations problems.

Although the principles of public relations are identical in Europe and America, the practical application in all cases must take into account local and national customs, traditions, attitudes, and many other special factors. This applies, of course, to all countries of the world. International trade is expanding and wherever business goes today, public relations problems are sure to follow.

The growth of international trade is inevitable in our civilization. The longing for the things that add to human comfort, and subtract from human misery and burden, is contagious—and it is spreading around the world. Even a slight improvement in the living standard of a sizeable portion of the world's rapidly increasing population will bring further increases in international trade. Unless civilization decides to commit suicide, this will bring better understanding among all the people touched by international trade.

But partly due to Russian propaganda, American diplomacy—which seeks understanding among nations—is distrusted and misunderstood in many parts of the world.

American business suffers from this circumstance. This places upon American companies engaged in foreign trade an added responsibility to strive for acceptance and goodwill in foreign lands.

To the extent that such efforts succeed, they will help advance the cause of international understanding. Thus, American business can play (and is playing) an important part in strengthening American diplomacy.

Obviously, American companies are under a handicap in some foreign environments because they are considered strangers in the community. Even in the sophisticated countries of Western Europe anti-American business attitudes sometimes crop up, especially in competitive situations.

There was a flare-up of anti-American business feelings in the United Kingdom some years ago following the Ford take-over of the outstanding shares of its British subsidiary. Current feelings in Europe seem to be directed against American business interests in the Common Market.

Within the Common Market the anti-American business

attitude is primarily caused by the political concept of General de Gaulle. This concept includes the theory that the continent of Europe is an historical and geographical entity of which "the Anglo-Saxons" are not part. Obviously this theory is finding a measure of support from other Europeans who see their self-interest served. There is a feeling among some Europeans that the Common Market they are building is primarily designed for their interest and not for the benefit of Americans, British, and others who are "outside."

Using American dimensions, American speed and American efficiency, spurred on by the astonishing speed of Europe's own economic growth and integration, American business has expanded its operations rapidly in the Common Market.

The size of the investments involved and the rapidity with which they have taken place have surprised and disconcerted many cautious and tradition-minded European elements, including some generally friendly towards the United States.

In dealing with these problems that pertain, of course, to all other areas outside of Europe too, it would seem to me that American business should consider the adoption of several policies that would be of real help:

1. There is a lack of business "diplomats." We simply do not have enough well-trained and experienced people who know enough about the foreign business climate. We should devise ways and means to train such people, although it may take years to bring them along, as it takes many years to develop career foreign-affairs officials.

2. In the meanwhile U.S. corporations should avail themselves of the best possible advisers that can be found locally in each of the countries involved. Public relations counsel should be used not only for usual services that they provide

but also for gathering and interpreting data on economic and political trends. This has been found of substantial value by some of the most forward-looking American companies in the international field.

3. Language training programs become increasingly important and should reward the companies now engaging in them.

4. Reporting facilities in foreign capitals and other nerve centers such as Geneva and Hong Kong should be established and/or improved. Most of our large companies maintain a Washington office for reporting and other purposes. For some strange reason no such facilities are maintained in foreign capitals by American companies with large interests at stake in those countries.

Naturally, international public relations is a two-way street in the sense that public relations activities carried on in the United States by other countries are helping our people to a better understanding of foreign ideas and viewpoints.

Thus, the contribution of international public relations goes far beyond commercial ambitions. Everywhere, it seems, there is a mounting desire to find ways of improving understanding between employees and employers, management and shareholders, plant and community, and between peoples across national borders.

Expansion of public relations activity is gradually developing on every continent and in every country of the free world. In Australia, New Zealand, The Philippines, Japan and South Africa—to mention only a few—countries and companies are giving increasing thought to the power of public opinion and to the need for public relations.

Public relations departments are being organized by industry, and public relations counseling firms are being established. Admittedly, a measure of caution persists, as with anything new and unfamiliar. Nevertheless, the trend is apparent nearly everywhere, and is most pronounced in Europe.

Although a great portion of our work in the international field is concerned with business enterprises, we have undertaken a number of assignments in other areas. For example, our firm has had a long relationship with The Development Board of Nassau for the promotion of that area as a vacation spot. It wasn't until 1950 that the British Colony of the Bahamas decided to go "big time" in promoting tourism, the only industry in the 700-island archipelago off the coast of Florida. The Bahamas Development Board, headed then as now by Stafford L. Sands, C.B.E., M.H.A., convinced the legislature that tourists had to be "purchased." This conviction eventually developed into a three-way program of advertising, sales and publicity-promotion.

Hill and Knowlton was given the responsibility in 1954 for publicity and promotion. In the ensuing years, the News Bureau in Nassau has grown into a bustling office of some twenty-five people, including specialists in fishing, yachting, hometown publicity, and its own photography department. Representatives in Miami and New York work in tandem with Nassau, maintaining contact with all news media in their areas.

The proof of the wisdom of the Bahamas Development Board's original decision—and its unswerving support of its tourist promotion program ever since—is found in figures compiled by the Immigration Department. In the late 1940s, about 30,000 vacationers visited Nassau—and only during the winter months. This figure has grown to approximately 400,000 in Nassau and the "Out Islands"—on a year-round basis.

According to official government estimates, each visitor spends $198 in the Bahamas, of which $68 is government revenue. The "cost" to the government in advertising, sales and publicity is just over $7 each—a pretty good "profit margin" for any kind of business.

The growth of public relations abroad will continue, I believe, to be uneven, but certain. In Europe, progress is rapid and the opportunities for public relations to help in the economic and social advancement are great. In the rest of the world, development may come more slowly, depending largely upon political and economic stability. I am mindful that public relations has been pictured by some people in this field as the ultimate solution to the international tensions that are keeping the world in its critical state of unrest. Such views are excessive and unrealistic. But I do believe public relations will play an important role in the momentous economic integration that is taking place in Europe and eventually must occur in other great sections of the world. In the process, the art of modern communications will be applied to an increasingly broad spectrum of international activity, contributing to the better development of understanding between peoples the world over.

The confidence of our firm in the future of international public relations has been certified by the establishment of a European Fellowship program under which each year an outstanding young European will be brought to the United States for a course in public relations subjects at a leading American university. Selection of the Fellowship students will be made by a committee of prominent Europeans, including Felix von Eckardt, presently West Germany's representative in West Berlin and previously official spokesman for the Adenauer government, and Senator Giuseppe Caron of Italy, formerly vice president of the European Common

Market Authority; Dr. C. L. W. Fock, The Netherlands; Mr. P. van der Rest, Président Groupement des Hauts-Fourneaux et Aciéries Belges, Belgium; and M. le Professeur Roland Ruffieux, Directeur de la Bibliothèque Nationale Suisse, Switzerland.

16

Hoover and Kennedy—a Study in Contrasts

A WRITER dealing with developments in public relations cannot avoid discussing the penetration of its skills into the halls of government and their use as presidential political tools. I have made a comparison of such efforts as far back as the term of Herbert Hoover. The result is a study in contrasts no less marked than the ideological differences that separate these two men who have held America's highest office.

Herbert Hoover's rise to the Presidency, his steep decline in the esteem of the American people in the wake of the Great Depression, and his subsequent long climb back to a beloved place in the hearts of his countrymen, is a fascinating saga.

In studying the career of Mr. Hoover, one is struck by the important part played by public relations both in his downgrading and in his later comeback over the years. The descent was planned and executed by his enemies; the ascent was planned in some measure by loyal friends. But largely the latter was the result of his own natural genius for public service at the highest level.

In 1928, soon after the Hoover election, the Democratic

National Committee set up an operation in Washington's National Press Building specifically charged with the task of discrediting the Hoover Administration and its head. Such effort on the part of political parties was not unheard of then although not as commonplace as today. After the depression hit, this operation was concentrated pitilessly upon a single purpose never paralleled in American life. There began, under the questionable genius of Charles Michelson, what was to become perhaps the most vicious, persistent, and effective smear-campaign ever conducted against any public man in American history.

Public relations also has played a leading role in the life of John F. Kennedy. Probably to a greater extent than anything else he did, it provided the key which opened for him the doors at 1600 Pennsylvania Avenue.

Three things have happened since Mr. Hoover's day to change the whole climate of White House public relations and communications:

1. The means of communication have proliferated. To newspapers and magazines have been added radio, television —glamorized and extended internationally with the globe-circling Telstar. Not only are there more media, but each carries far more information to the people, faster and more effectively. Television now brings the personal presence of a President right into the nation's living rooms. The impact is incalculable.

2. America is the strongest nation in a bitter global cold war with communism. Whatever its President says and does has instant significance around the world. This rostrum—constantly spotlighted for the nation and the world—represents both awesome opportunity and terrible responsibility.

3. Mr. Kennedy is a politician born and bred with an intuitive and never-sleeping sense of the importance of wooing public favor. He not only has the means of communica-

tion and the platform at his disposal, he has the astuteness for making the most of them, at least where verbal persuasion is concerned.

Two major points of dissimilarity mark the public relations of the Hoover and Kennedy administrations. First, Mr. Hoover's term predated the vast "public information" apparatus that since has become a fixed part of our Federal government. Second, Mr. Hoover himself, with his background as an engineer, businessman, and non-political public servant, lacked the public relations flair that is one of President Kennedy's attributes.

The two men had one great crisis in common. Early in the administrations of each there was a devastating collapse on Wall Street. The first was Black Friday of October 26, 1929, and the second was the equally black Monday of May 28, 1962. These catastrophes confronted both presidents with crises calling for prompt action.

Although Mr. Kennedy was blamed for unsettling business and financial sentiment by moves like his angry attack on steel companies for raising their prices, it is unlikely that what he did brought the worldwide securities decline in the spring of 1962.

It is equally illogical to hold Mr. Hoover responsible for the Black Friday of 1929. The perspective of time has made it clear that the calamity was the aftermath of destructive global forces generated in World War I. President Hoover happened to be in the White House when those forces erupted with the sudden violence of a volcano.

Mr. Hoover lost no time in taking action. He moved to reduce taxes. He called business leaders together to make a concerted fight against wage cuts, unemployment, and erosion of business and public morale. In many areas of the economy he sought to develop and carry out emergency measures that would contribute to a sound recovery, including public works and aid to farmers. However, many of Mr. Hoover's plans were blocked by his political opposition.

During the crucial period from the election day of November 5, 1932, to Franklin D. Roosevelt's inauguration on March 4, 1933, the incumbent President sought in vain to meet with his successor. He wanted to obtain support in pushing through the Democratic Congress some recovery legislation of utmost importance to the nation and on which every day's delay meant a deeper depression and a more painful recovery. Apparently for political reasons, Mr. Roosevelt held himself inaccessible to the Chief Executive during these four final months of his term.

It is for the economists to determine the degree to which America's financial problems during this chaotic period were heightened by Mr. Roosevelt's attitude. Of more immediate significance to our discussion is the knowledge that Mr. Hoover did little to take his case to the people or to use the power of the Presidency to portray to the press the importance of the steps he recommended. Those who lament the overuse of government public relations today must in fairness see that the country then suffered from a reverse extreme in which the forces of communication of that day lay largely unused.

During his term Mr. Hoover made no talks to the people by radio. He made few public addresses. On appropriate occasions he issued White House statements to the press. The "White House spokesman" was invented by President Coolidge. Neither he nor any of his predecessors had a press secretary. This adornment was introduced by President Franklin D. Roosevelt—with Steve Early—as was the broadcast "Fireside Chat." Mr. Hoover had only a few press conferences during his term, and there was no well-organized effort to mobilize public opinion at any time.

During the years 1930 to 1932, President Hoover in fact

refused to take time from his preoccupation with the country's fateful problems to counterattack the prodigious campaign of vilification aimed at him. He did not, as we have noted, have the facilities that are available today for quickly reaching the entire American people. Public communication was almost entirely through the press. But even if all the modern tools of communication had been available to him, it is doubtful if Mr. Hoover would have used them to engage in a public contest of vituperation.

He was, as he is today, a man of unshakeable personal dignity. He never believed that words alone—eloquent or otherwise—represented accomplishment. He believed that if his policies and deeds served to keep America safe, basically strong, and above all *free* during its passage through crises, the ultimate judgment of his fellow man would be honest and fair. His confidence, of course, has been confirmed.

All he has said and done since leaving the White House, had it been carefully planned or calculated, would add up to a major achievement in public relations. But insofar as Mr. Hoover himself is concerned, I am sure there was no conscious planning. However, I am equally sure Mr. Hoover was well aware and warmly appreciative of the fact that he had numberless dedicated friends and admirers who have been determined to do everything possible to identify him affirmatively with the American people.

Many of these men, who have always referred to Mr. Hoover as "The Chief," were his able young assistants in World War I and Belgian relief days. Others among his devoted friends have included leaders of the press and radio such as Lowell Thomas, Roy Howard, H. V. Kaltenborn, Neil MacNeil, Alan Gould, Ray Henle, Reuben Maury, Walter Trohan, Richard Berlin, George Sokolsky, Mark Sullivan, Forrest Davis, and Frank Kent.

After the stock market crash in 1962, Mr. Kennedy began,

much as Mr. Hoover had done, by reassuring business and the investing public. He said he favored sound business progress as essential to the nation's economic growth. He noted that the government, with a 52 per cent share in industry's profits, has an enormous vested interest in the country's prosperity—in a vigorous private economy.

Like Mr. Hoover, he recommended a tax cut. He suggested public works programs. He asked for reform measures to curb "irresponsible" selling of stocks.

A major difference is that Mr. Hoover saw restoration of public confidence in the private sector of the economy as the prime goal. Mr. Kennedy seemed to see public acceptance of an expanding government role in the economy as the key solution. We cannot know what the fruits of Mr. Hoover's program might have been. It remains to be seen what Mr. Kennedy will accomplish. And if our final impression is cloudy, it will trace to his own performance and not to what others may do to misrepresent him in the public mind. Thanks to television, a firsthand view of our President at work has lost all novelty; and his contact with the nation's press is far greater than even FDR ever dreamed of.

When Franklin Roosevelt was President, the Washington press corps was small enough to be invited into the oval office of the Chief Executive for news conferences. By 1952, however, the ranks had swelled to the point where Dwight Eisenhower had to hold his press conferences outside the White House. Ike held 193 such meetings during his two terms and answered 5,766 individual press questions in the Indian Treaty Room of the Executive Office Building next door to the Mansion. The 300-seat capacity of the Indian Treaty Room was outgrown by the time Mr. Kennedy took office and the press-conference scene was shifted to the Auditorium in the New State Department Building.

Eisenhower was the first of America's presidents to permit

direct quotes and completely unedited transcripts of his Wednesday morning conferences with the press. Except for this concession, however, he—like Mr. Hoover—had short patience for intrusions in his workday of matters pertaining solely to the press or to public opinion.

John F. Kennedy has far out-paced all predecessors in his willingness even anxiousness, to live and work in the full focus of public attention. Not since the early years of the Roosevelt Presidency has press membership been such a key to White House friendship. The Kennedys spent the night before his inauguration at a Georgetown party for members of the press. At their first unofficial White House dinner party, press accreditation was the common denominator that linked most of the guests.

Mr. Kennedy has permitted interviews with members of his family, pictorial stories about his children, their pets and playmates, and he has posed for, or permitted use of, portrait shots for the cover of nearly every major magazine. At the newsstand in the Solar Building that houses Hill and Knowlton's Washington offices, I once counted twenty-one magazines with a picture of President Kennedy or a member of his family on the cover.

In the spring of 1961 the President of the United States modeled a two-button suit on the cover of *Gentleman's Quarterly*, a men's fashion magazine. This was no candid shot exploited without the President's consent. Inside was a full acknowledgment to Mr. Kennedy for graciously taking time from his busy day to pose for a *Gentleman's Quarterly* photographer.

President Kennedy's availability to a select group of the press has made possible firsthand reports of the problems and goals of a Chief Executive as never before *during* incumbency. In the *Saturday Evening Post*, Mr. Kennedy as President Kennedy, personally by-lined an article for the American reader.

As members of a national citizenship foundation, a group of my friends visited with President Kennedy in February, 1962. During their meeting the President told them of some of the collateral duties of his post. With all he had on his mind that day, he lamented, he had had to spend nearly an hour with a *Life* magazine reporter. It is hard to conceive of any of the Kennedy predecessors having the patience or finding the time to meet with one reporter to develop a single article, even in a medium of *Life*'s impressive influence. As a matter of fact, it is not always easy to persuade one of today's corporate giants to take time out for an interview with a member of the fourth estate.

The President not only talks with individual newsmen, but he particularly likes to meet with small groups of editors and publishers. As a one-time newspaper man himself, he appreciates the great value of explaining his views firsthand to the press. This is a well-known and sound public relations procedure.

An Eisenhower official once told me that a sure way to kill a proposal in an Eisenhower cabinet meeting was to tell the President the proposition's main virtue was that it would be politically advantageous or would increase his popularity with the public. Eisenhower granted no private audiences with individual members of the press, fiercely guarded his grandchildren from pictures and publicity, and limited Mrs. Eisenhower to an occasional picture for a philanthropy like the Heart Fund or the March of Dimes.

When Franklin Roosevelt developed his famed fireside chats, he brought government-to-people communications to a new level. A good measure of how personally his listener took his messages was gained when Roosevelt one evening suggested citizens write to him and share their problems and advice. A mountain of mailbags descended on the White House. They were stacked ceiling high in the rooms of the East Wing, and it was some weeks before official mail could be sorted from the folksy notes sent in by would-be Presidential pen pals.

The Kennedy Administration has originated a plan to bring the government-public contact even closer. Across the nation it has staged citizens' conferences where speakers present the Administration views on pending legislation.

In Franklin Roosevelt's days in the White House, members of his staff were instructed that they were to be neither seen nor heard. In the absence of such a specific mandate, the natural inclination of the members of an administration is to follow the lead of the Chief Executive. Eisenhower kept his relations with the press and his communications with the public businesslike, formal. Members of his top officialdom took their cue from the President, guarding against publicity and at all costs flamboyance.

Conversely, under Mr. Kennedy, it should not surprise us to see members of his Cabinet and staff not only much in the news but occasionally stretching for the right prop or contriving the right situation to make their actions newsworthy. The Presidential press consciousness obviously has hit all corners of his administration like a contagion when it can be considered within the bounds of Cabinet dignity for Interior Secretary Udall to open a new national park by donning skin-diving gear to cut an underwater ribbon. This history-making performance occurred on March 18, 1962 at Buck Island Reef Park, St. Croix, Virgin Islands.

The depth of the penetration of that news consciousness was apparent late in the summer of 1963, when the Office of Comptroller of the Currency began publication of *The National Banking Review, a Journal of Policy and Practice.* Its purpose was to afford this previously unheard voice of government "a medium for the expression of views."

The public and press relations activity of the federal government as a whole has become a colossus of unmeasured proportions. Virtually every bureau, agency, commission, department and legislative office in Washington has its public relations or publicity department, many with large staffs, and all devoted to getting their stories told. Their main purpose is to keep the public informed on government activities and services, although in some cases their work is obviously affected by political motivation.

The Kennedy Administration has worked more assiduously with more evidently conscious planning on its public relations than any previous administration in our history. Perhaps this is one of the indications that public relations is coming of age. The result is that President Kennedy has been called "America's No. 1 unhidden persuader," and a poll in Congress gave him a higher rating for public relations than for any other single ability. The nation's press has taken to giving almost as much attention to his public relations effort as to any other facet of his activity.

Not all of this public discussion, of course, has been favorable. Despite the skill with which the Administration has sought to work in this field, an outburst of criticism of its alleged "managed news" policy developed early in 1963. The controversy came into full bloom on March 18, 1963, when a House Government Operations Subcommittee began hearings on these charges.

A further shock came in a bluntly critical article by Arthur Krock, famed Washington correspondent of *The New York Times* in the March, 1963, issue of *Fortune* magazine. Mr. Krock declared that there was a "managed news policy" in Washington and that it was employed more cynically and boldly than ever before in the country's peacetime history. He held that the policy was exercised directly through suppression, concealment and distortion of news, and indirectly through "coloring" of news or influencing its form of presentation through "social flattery" of correspondents, and other means. Mr. Krock's fifty years of experience as a newspaperman gave his views great weight.

Certainly Mr. Kennedy is a past master at using to the utmost for his own purposes what Mr. Krock calls the "awesome aura" of the White House. This is the chief instrument of the Administration's so-called "management of news." But I fully concur with Mr. Krock that if writers, radio and TV commentators, and editors are unduly influenced by this flattering attention from on high, the onus is on them and not on the flatterer.

Other critical appraisals by respected journalists continued to reflect deep concern. Hanson Baldwin, the veteran military analyst and writer of *The New York Times*, declared in the April, 1963, *Atlantic* magazine that "there is a major question about the methods employed in the Administration's public relations policies . . ." Mr. Baldwin said the New Frontier had produced, in the opinion of many newsmen, "some astonishing examples of news repression and distortion, management and control, and pressures and propaganda." Robert J. Donovan, chief Washington correspondent of the *New York Herald Tribune*, observed that: "Judged by the advance standards of Kennedy techniques in public imagery, Madison Avenue isn't paved yet." Alan L. Otten of the *Wall Street Journal* has suggested that the Administration's news often is more "mismanaged" than "managed." In other words, news stories do not always turn out as hoped for by the "managers." Like Mr. Krock and Mr. Baldwin, Mr. Otten too has found conspicuous the President's personal efforts to flatter and influence selected columnists and broadcasters.

But it is not only newsmen who are mesmerized by the glamor of the White House, and Mr. Kennedy is not the first occupant to discover this is so. During the reign of FDR, I knew an important industrialist of the hate-Roosevelt school whose face would redden as his voice choked with rage when he talked of the President. But one fine day he was invited to the White House. He accepted the invitation and spent an hour and a half alone with Mr. Roosevelt. He came out a changed man. I saw him a few days later with a group of his cronies in industry, trying desperately and unsuccessfully to tell them that "he isn't so bad after all!"

No one reasonably can object to the fact that President Kennedy is utilizing every tool at hand to accomplish his aims. The main concern is that these aims be good for the whole country and not simply alluring to certain large voting groups. In our form of society, the President has not only the right but the duty to solicit the consent of the governed, which is to say, to explain his goals to the people and to seek their support by all appropriate means.

In the light of subsequent events, it is apparent that President Hoover did not go to the people often enough. Certainly Mr. Kennedy cannot be criticized on this score. But there are two sides to the coin of public relations—words and deeds. President Hoover gave greatest weight to deeds. There are some who believe that President Kennedy's reliance on words may at times blunt the sharp edge of action. James Reston of *The New York Times* has observed that it is "easier to write messages than to draft programs to implement the messages."

President Kennedy has called eloquently for "action" to move America forward. But what happens to the American economy will depend not so much upon words and urgings but upon the soundness of policies designed to stimulate private enterprise and release the energies of the people. Will the roadblocks be removed in time for business, as *Fortune* magazine has put it, to invest fast enough to employ the nation's resources adequately?

In short, Mr. Kennedy's case will rest not on skillful persuasion alone but on the extent to which action is suited to his verbal assurances of faith in the private enterprise system.

Like his idol, Franklin D. Roosevelt, he uses lavishly the techniques of persuasive communications. But the years appear to be dimming the image of Roosevelt as an economic rescuer in the light of data showing federal deficits ranging from 19.4 billion dollars to 40 billion dollars during his first eight years while unemployment never fell below 8 million until Hitler started his war in 1939.

Mr. Hoover had no such facility as either Mr. Roosevelt or Mr. Kennedy for communicating with the people, but the integrity of his determination to preserve the nation without jeopardizing its fundamental institutions looms larger by the year.

We do not know how history will position Mr. Kennedy. But we do know that what he does, far more than what he says, will go far to decide the rise or fall of the American economy in the years ahead.

17

Industry-Education Cooperation: INVESTMENT IN THE FUTURE

DURING the thirties and forties American Iron and Steel Institute and other clients of my firm, along with many other organizations, were sending printed materials of various kinds to schools throughout the country. It was hoped that these could be of use to teachers as classroom aids.

But one day in 1948 I was startled when a friend from Toledo told me he had seen a large school storage room piled high with such materials unopened, unused and gathering dust. Why, I wondered, should educators be so disinterested in such efforts to help them? The answer at which I arrived was, in fact, simple. It was that most of this literature represented what the producers *thought* the teachers wanted. No one that I could discover actually had taken the trouble to find out from teachers what *they* wanted, if anything.

I went to Walter Tower of the Steel Institute and proposed a nationwide survey to study the problem. He saw the need at once, gave his approval, and the project that resulted was the beginning of the education department of Hill and Knowlton, a department that remains to this day, I believe, the only education section of a public relations counseling firm staffed by professional educators.

As a first step, we located a competent educator-research man who devised and carried out the survey we had in mind. Altogether the study required two years and covered nearly five thousand school administrators and teachers. When the results were in, we could see clearly that industry thinking in this field had to change. Even so, the principal finding should have surprised no one.

It was that a real need existed for industry-supplied information in the schools, but that the material, to be widely used, must be prepared in cooperation with schoolmen themselves. It must be planned not simply *for* teachers but *with* them.

Nine out of ten of the teachers surveyed told us they would use sponsored materials in the classroom *if these were objectively presented.* Their greatest need, they reported, was for up-to-date information not ordinarily available in textbooks. A school program suited to the requirements of an industrialized society, they felt, should draw liberally on business and industry as sources of teaching materials.

But in calling for "objectivity," they were insisting upon materials specifically designed for educational use. And such materials must be available on request where and in the quantity necessary for the teachers' most efficient employment of them.

Two facts were obvious to me at this point: 1. that industry-education cooperation would become increasingly important for the steel industry and, for that matter, for many other industries; and 2. that we must add professional educators to our staff if the firm was to be of real help in this field.

Thus we employed professional educators to carry out various projects over the next several years. Dr. Warren Nelson, whose doctoral project at Columbia University Teachers College had in fact been our two-year survey of educator views, helped launch several industry-education cooperative ventures. He is now a professor of education at Miami University in Oxford, Ohio. He was assisted by Dr. Amo de Bernardis, who is now assistant superintendent of schools in Portland, Oregon.

In 1953 I met a young educator who had been a teacher, principal and superintendent of schools in the state of Washington and had recently come East as associate director of the Joint Council on Economic Education. His understanding of the problems of economic education and his views on what proper industry cooperation could accomplish impressed me. I persuaded him to join us and he has directed our education department since that time.

In this post, Dr. Albert L. Ayars has helped to pioneer some important and far-reaching industry-education programs. At the same time, he has maintained a high level of general professional activity. He is the author of a number of books and articles and has written extensively for education journals. He has served as a visiting professor at major universities and has been active in many societies and associations, including service as president of the Council of National Organizations for Adult Education, of the Business-Industry Section of the National Science Teachers Association, and of Association Internationale des Étudiants en Sciences Économiques et Commerciales-United States, sponsor of a major international student-exchange program. He has served on numerous national consultative and advisory committees of educators formed to recommend improvements in American education.

I have identified Dr. Ayars at some length to illustrate the extent to which modern public relations has become diversified in its service. Experienced specialists are required to handle its many facets, among the most significant of which is industry-education cooperation.

In 1956 Dr. Bertis E. Capehart joined the firm as associate director of the education department. He had been superintendent of schools in Oak Ridge, Tennessee, and—like Dr. Ayars—had been active in university and public school teaching, writing, and organizational service.

It is interesting also that twelve account executives on the present Hill and Knowlton staff are qualified as teachers. Ten have taught in colleges and universities. Our president, Bert C. Goss, holds a doctoral degree and for several years was a professor of economics at New York University. And while these men do not presume to be experts in education, their experience unquestionably is helpful in numerous programs on which they work, including many involving cooperative efforts with educators.

Following our original study in 1950, a program of information created by educators themselves was submitted to high educational authorities by American Iron and Steel Institute, and it received complete approval. Only then was it offered to schools—with a success that has brought it into widening use each succeeding year.

The program recognizes that, in producing materials, business management is the authority for accuracy of the information; but the educational advisers weigh its pertinency to the age group being addressed, its usefulness for teaching purposes, and the manner of presentation.

Our research convinced us also that industry could contribute more than classroom teaching aids. We learned that teachers were eager to gain for themselves firsthand knowledge of industry's work.

As one answer to this need, we developed a plan whereby teachers and business people could get together to study the industrial resources in their own community. The Steel Institute in 1952 joined with local educators, community groups, and nearby Miami University to sponsor the first Community Resources Workshop in Hamilton, Ohio. One of the Institute's company members, Armco Steel of Middletown, Ohio, lent active cooperation to this project. It was a pilot effort to determine whether such a program would be sufficiently productive to undertake on a broader scale. At its conclusion, there appeared to be no doubts in the minds of any of the participants. Since that time, more than fifty workshops have been held in all parts of the country and in Canada and Mexico. At this writing, plans are made for two Central American sessions, in Honduras and Costa Rica, to be attended both by native educators and teachers in American schools there.

Many teachers in our elementary and secondary schools take summer courses in higher institutions of learning. A Community Resources Workshop is supported financially by industries in the area, as part of the summer curriculum in a university or college, and the participants receive graduate or undergraduate credit. The general purpose is for educators to explore community resources available to them and how they can use them in their teaching. Projects focus around the various activities of local industries, government agencies, courts of law, parks and museums, and other important institutions. Field trips are made to study industrial plants and other sources of useful information.

The collateral benefits to the teacher are many. In studying the work of a large industrial organization, for example, the high-school teacher can get a close-up view of mathematics at work in engineering, of physics and chemistry applied in the laboratory, of English as used in communications, of economics as it lays down the operating law everywhere.

The net result of the workshops is to help develop more

effective teachers, to help the schools draw upon the community strength for educational improvement, and to bring about greater school and community agreement on educational aims.

In establishing an education department, I also had another, more specific problem in mind. It was the feeling—held by many others as well, of course—that a great part of the American people lacked real understanding of the American economic system. I had the feeling that students were not learning much about the economics of the private enterprise system in their schools. My thought was not that they were being misinformed so much as that they were not being exposed to substantive information on this subject.

An education department gave us a vehicle for studying these doubts—to see to what extent they were justified, if at all. One of our first studies concluded that fundamental economic concepts are developed by pupils before they reach high school. Subsequent surveys indicated that these concepts, for the most part, remain shallow—that most high-school students do not understand our economic system or how it operates. (On this point, note also Chapter 13.)

A 1960 study by Opinion Research Corporation confirmed that typical freshmen entering college have little knowledge of the facts and principles required to understand how our economic system works. The study demonstrated further that college students gained the desired economic fundamentals only when they studied the subject. When quizzed on economic facts or principles, students who had studied economics came out on top, showing a much better understanding of our system's underlying concepts of productivity, capital formation, and pricing.

The popular notion that college teaching of economics breeds socialist leanings in students, incidentally, is not borne out by such studies. Intensive work in economics in college generally leads students toward ideological positions not unfavorable to the private enterprise system. Moreover, other research—principally by Dr. Willys R. Knight of Georgia State College of Business Administration—has indicated that students tend to become more "conservative" (generally speaking, favorable to private enterprise and opposed to government paternalism) as they progress toward graduation. The same research has shown that good students tend to be more sympathetic to business' role in our system, and poor ones lean "more toward government paternalism in economic affairs."

Those findings, however, represent only *relative* levels of understanding. By and large, as I have already suggested, the adult population is uneducated in terms of familiarity with the principles of our economic system. By noting that some 5 per cent of high-school students now take a course in economics, that 40 per cent of high-school graduates go to college, and that one-fourth of the college students take an economics course, we arrive at the fact that only one out of every ten adult citizens has studied as much as a single course in economics.

All of these findings suggest that students, beginning in the elementary grades, need to receive a broader base of economic information in their school work.

A recent study by Dr. Ayars of leading economics textbooks used in high schools showed that there are no important gaps in the economic content of these books. Textbooks in other courses, however, give little attention of real substance to economics. The study therefore concludes, and educators have generally agreed, that there is urgent need and opportunity for curriculum enrichment from properly prepared outside materials on economics. Industry, at the heart of our private enterprise system, ought to be a basic source of these materials.

Opinion Research Corporation in 1955 reported that, in special programs where industry had made an effort to work closely with school authorities, students absorbed and retained many of the ideas covered. High-school boys and girls who participated in cooperative industry programs in three test cities showed considerably higher scores on an economics quiz than those who did not take part. Other studies at other levels have developed similar results.

Our experiences, and those of many others, have shown that companies can assist at all levels, not only in providing objective materials but in a number of other ways. They can afford opportunities to teachers and students for firsthand observation of industry and business in action. They can furnish case-in-point examples to help lend reality and excitement to what many students otherwise are apt to consider a dry and abstract subject.

Of increasing importance and value, business can help to sponsor workshops, conferences, and seminars in economics for teachers themselves. But this is not, I should point out, the province of business alone. The AFL-CIO helps to finance economic education workshops for teachers, professors and clergymen. Several foundations sponsor programs in this field. I would say, however, that American corporate management has a major responsibility in this area of education cooperation, entailing its own security and advancement as well as the general public interest.

College professors of economics and business in recent years have expressed the desire for face-to-face discussion of industry's problems with industry executives. In the late 1950s we questioned a large number of professors and deans of economics, who told us they would benefit from hearing frank talk by business executives about their economic problems and their industry's points of view. The educators added, properly, that they should be given the opportunity to discuss and criticize what they heard with the industry people. Then, they said, the information they gleaned could be put to practical use in their teaching.

Against this background the first Steel Industry Economics Seminar for College Professors was held in Youngstown, Ohio, in November of 1960. The seminar, planned jointly by the area educators and the Steel Institute, brought favorable reactions from both groups. Others have followed in other locations each summer. Each meeting is for two days. A leading university acts as host, inviting usually about thirty deans and professors from nearby schools. The Steel Institute pays the expenses of the host institution and the participating educators. With fifteen to twenty industry people participating, business speakers present specific problems and views in considerable detail; small-group question and answer sessions then are led by professors; and finally there is general discussion based on panel reports of the small groups.

As I have indicated, the educators have told us that the seminars were valuable to them and that more should be held; they have found the results useful in teaching; they felt no restriction in freedom of expression; and they have found industry people frank and forthright in their answers to searching questions.

Industry executives, for their part, have been nearly unanimous in their opinion that the seminars provide an effective means of two-way communications with an important group of opinion leaders. They feel that these meetings help to create an atmosphere of sympathetic understanding.

In 1962, two others of our industry clients decided to embark on similar seminar programs. They were the Aerospace Industries Association and the Pharmaceutical Manufacturers Association, both representing industries of key importance in the American economy.

Industry should not, of course, seek to overburden the

summer schedules of economics and business educators. But there are some two thousand colleges and universities in the United States and it is obvious that a great many more such meetings could be held annually without even getting around to all professors who might be interested. I feel strongly that it would be to the benefit of all private enterprise, as well as to our educational system, if more industries would undertake projects of a like nature.

This is not to say that business leaders generally are ignoring the nation's educational needs. The evidence is to the contrary. It is true, of course, that many years ago most businessmen were indifferent toward education and educators, regarding this field as something outside their active sphere of interest. And too often those who did take an interest proved to be motivated by desire to use the schools for putting product promotion or other strictly self-interest material into the classrooms.

I can remember more than one corporate publicity manager who was astounded when I told him that his plans to persuade teachers to put straight-product literature into their pupils' hands—in the guise of marketing, research, or manufacturing illustrations—would create only ill will for his company.

Today a new spirit prevails. There is broad cooperation and greatly improved understanding between education and industry. Enlightened management, guided by sound public relations principles, has learned to think in terms of aiding education. And this aid given freely and without overtones of commercial exploitation is warmly welcomed.

Business leaders in ever-widening degree are giving of their talents and abilities toward the solution of our school problems. Men like Frank Abrams, former chairman of Standard Oil of New Jersey; Alfred E. Sloan, of General Motors; and others who formed the Citizens' Commission for the Public

Schools have devoted much time to it. Former Secretary of Defense Neil McElroy, while president of Procter & Gamble, was chairman of the White House Conference on Education. Now chairman of the Board of the company, he continues a deep and active interest in education.

Men like these have given much time to speeches before influential audiences and to articles in national publications urging aid to education. And throughout the country thousands of businessmen are serving on citizens' school committees and on school boards in their communities.

In terms of financial aid, contributions by business to institutions of higher learning and to their students rose from an estimated 40 million dollars in 1950 to about 160 million dollars in 1961. Higher education is receiving an increasingly larger share of the total corporate gift dollars. Assuming that business prosperity is maintained, the volume of corporate support for education undoubtedly will continue to rise. While industry's interest in research, in technology, and in developing well-trained engineers is reflected in these gifts, management's recognition of the value of liberal arts training is equally evident. To liberal arts colleges, for instance, went over 40 per cent or $1,216,000 of the 1961 grant by U.S. Steel Foundation.

Procter & Gamble, whose current annual grants exceed one and a quarter million dollars, was one of the first large companies to include women's colleges among its list of grantees. In announcing its general scholarship program several years ago, the company said:

> Both idealistic and practical reasons prompt Procter & Gamble's decision to launch its new scholarship program. Idealistically, we feel a social responsibility to do our share toward providing the increased opportunity that higher education gives American youth.

> Practically, we know that higher education brings with it a fuller understanding of how and why the private enterprise system operates to provide for all of us the higher standards of living which we enjoy. Also, we know the colleges supply the reservoir of talent upon which industry must depend for continued progress.

This statement in fact leads directly into conclusions upon which I would put the most serious emphasis. Many times in the past I have been asked: "Why should a company spend the money and executive time involved in all these activities? Why produce printed materials in great volume, why sponsor educator meetings, and why contribute large sums of money when you are unable to show any direct and measurable returns to the company from all this?"

We are not upset by such questions. It is important, in a free economy, for stockholders and interested citizens to inquire whether a corporation's money is being wisely spent or invested. But I believe that answers can be offered which throw a strong and heartening light on the whole function of the American corporation in today's society.

Management's prime goals are the preservation and progress of private enterprise. It can work for these goals only in a social order in which the majority of the people approve the private enterprise system. If this approval is to be preserved, it is to management's advantage to help budding citizens understand the vital function of business and industry in the community's life. This assistance is essential at all levels of education.

In the college and the university, management comes into a sphere that is just as influential as the banker's or the politician's in shaping the course of public opinion and the patterns of American ideological determination. The building and nourishing of close contact with the educational world is therefore as vital to business as anything it can do over the long range.

These are the more apparent answers. There are others, deeply underlying the whole complex of our way of living, to which educators and business leaders are giving their most thoughtful attention.

Increasingly we have come to realize that America has no more important asset than a well-educated citizenry. Our country's future depends to a large extent upon how well our schools, colleges, and universities prepare young people to meet the multiplex problems of our times. I am sure that that statement would have been true at any time over the past 100 years of our history, but never could it have been so valid as now, when the entire world is going through a nuclear-powered revolution that is changing scientific, political, and social processes with every new day and shows no sign at all of abatement.

Because our system of education is at the core of our security and progress as a nation in the midst of this great revolution, all Americans and all American institutions have deep responsibilities for maintaining and improving it. Business should and will grow voluntarily as one of the most active of these institutions.

Public relations has been of value to corporate management in its steps to meet these responsibilities to date. I am sure that sound public relations policies and actions will continue to guide the broader industry-education cooperation of the future.

18

What Is the Public Interest?

"*. . . This will enable the business man to obtain advice in advance without litigation as to whether a proposed merger would be regarded as contrary to* the public interest . . ."

"*. . . The* public interest *in major wage and price determination is substantial. Ways must be found to bring* that public interest *before the parties concerned in a fair and orderly manner . . .*"

"*. . . This bill serves the* public interest. *It involves the govern ment because it involves the public welfare . . .*"

THE above three quotations are from statements by the President of the United States. Picked out at random, they are but three of scores of examples of his use of the term, "the public interest," in his public messages and utterances.

No one of course has more reason to be concerned with "the public interest" than the President of the country, but we see abundant evidence every day that he is far from alone in keeping this remarkable phrase hard at work. I am constantly impressed by the number of times you will encounter the term in the course of a day's reading. "The public interest" is invoked by both governmental and non-governmental people; the context of its use may be legal, quasi-legal, political, social, economic or theological. I have been especially intrigued by the fact that its implication is brought to bear on current problems by leading citizens in almost all walks of life, often holding opposite points of view.

Government regulatory bodies advance "the public interest" as not only the supreme but virtually the sole standard for making judgments. The chairman of the Federal Trade Commission, Paul Rand Dixon, has declared: "Private rights are important but *the public interest* is a greater right." Rupert L. Murphy, member of the Interstate Commerce Commission, has pointed out that: "The term 'public interest' pervades the whole of the Interstate Commerce Act."

But critics of government officials clearly claim equal right to the use of the term. Thus David Lawrence, the editor of the *U.S. News & World Report,* asking editorially, in the issue of September 3, 1962, "Do we really like a President who is a politician?" writes:

> May we hope that someday a President of the United States will present the image of a man who, in behalf of the American people, has taken the vows of self-sacrifice and fearless devotion solely to *the public interest.* (Italics added.)

So, again and again, we come across this pervasive term as it is applied to public discussion and debate, often involving some of the most trenchant issues of our time. It is employed to justify, to appeal, to accuse, to deny, to judge, to arouse, to explain, and more.

We might expect that the phrase would wear out from overwork—that we should have come before now to consider it hackneyed and trite. Other similar expressions seem to have lost much of their potency with usage. "The common good," "the general welfare," and even to some extent "the national interest," found most often in the context of international issues, are examples.

But the fact is that the efficacy of "the public interest" does not fade. It very often comes at us from the spoken or written message with a peculiar force that we may not be able to explain but that we strongly feel. It probably is true that today there is no more curious, mystical, frustrating and yet important phrase in the English language.

If this were not the case, we should hardly find this term being put to such extensive and unabated use by people who otherwise are quick to sense when a word or a phrase, grown commonplace, has lost its capacity to effect a response. Aside from the fact that "the public interest" is imbedded in our legal and regulatory language, most serious attention is given to it by our educators, editors and other leading professional people; by our most articulate statesmen and leaders in business, labor and other fields of private and public life.

Obviously it is a concept to which the public relations counselor must give increasing reflection. Business managements are concerned with the problems of conducting their corporate or industry affairs in ways that they may feel are contributive to public progress. They must arrive at effective policies that go far beyond their economic and operating functions into the complex realms of social, governmental and political relationships. The large majority push forward into these policy areas as a matter of choice. But in terms of the long-range survival of corporate enterprise, there is little choice involved; it is a matter of essentiality.

Dr. Henry S. Kariel, writing on "The Corporation and the Public Interest" in the September, 1962, *Annals of the American Academy of Political and Social Science*, observes that "the case for more thoroughgoing state action [on regulation of corporate enterprise] has been made with increasing cogency during the last two decades." And he draws the point:

> Since corporations are institutionally incapable of making policy in reference to standards other than those of efficiency and economy, so the criticism runs, the state will have to act. It may either supervise them so that social values will be introduced or else it may break them into fragments so that the classical competitive market will automatically take care of social value . . .
>
> . . . If, then, both socialization and fragmentation are undesirable—that is, if the large-scale business corporation is to be maintained as a viable entity—corporate managers themselves will have to consider non-technological and non-economic factors as they make their decisions. At a price that has not yet been discussed, they will have to consider the public interest.

Business and other non-governmental institutions, then, face insistent problems of determining where the public interest lies and what needs to be done to serve it accurately. In the process, they face equally important tasks in communications, for support of their policies will grow largely as they are able to strengthen public understanding of both their competence to recognize what *is* in the public interest and their desire to align their policies accordingly.

Hereupon we arrive at a central and critical question. It is a question that underlies much of the debate and decision of our time, but one for which no generally suitable answer has been found. What indeed *do* we mean by "the public interest"? What does *anyone*—in or out of government—mean when he invokes "the public interest"?

Is the concept definable at all? If so, what is its definition?

What are the criteria that determine whether something is or is not in the public interest? And who is best qualified to make the decision?

M. R. Lefkoe, writing in the *Financial Analysts Journal* of July-August, 1962, declares "It is a phrase which is used by all, and understood by none." The head of a Federal regulatory body asserts: "Nowhere is there to be found a wholly acceptable definition."

Most widely quoted, undoubtedly, is the Jeremy Bentham postulate of "the greatest good for the greatest number." But this is a generalization that tends to leave some basic concomitant questions unanswered. For one, we are moved immediately to ask, "*Who* and *what* decides that which is 'the greatest good'?" We may also inquire: "Does 'the public interest,' then, automatically countenance what is not good for the lesser number?"

The courts have wrestled with the "public interest" problem many times but never have succeeded in coming up with a workable definition. We know that Congress assigns to Federal commissions the authority to regulate industry in "the public interest." But the interpretation of the phrase is largely left to the discretion of the members of each specific commission.

ICC Commissioner Murphy, in a speech at Atlanta, Georgia, in September, 1957, presented a most illuminating and forthright discussion of this subject. He said, in part:

> It is peculiar to the administrative process that while the evidence of record in each proceeding is for the most part objective, the "public interest" as a standard of judgment is inherently subjective. Subject only to review by the courts, the application of the standard is characterized by the large measure of discretion enjoyed by responsible civil servants in arriving at findings and conclusions.

And, referring to "the greatest good for the greatest number" tenet, Mr. Murphy said:

> At best this is a generalization useful solely for the purpose of giving direction to thinking in the abstract. The actual application involves much more than can be stated by definition and, as adapted to any given factual situation, it is necessary to take into consideration other important cumulative forces such as the individual backgrounds of the civil servants, personal connotations, usages and practices of the regulated industry, Congressional policies, specific provisions of the statutes, and court decisions; and, *when finally a course of action is decided upon, it may be a response to nothing more convincing that a feeling or an impression.* (Italics mine.)

Even considering this subjective latitude, if determinations of the public interest were restricted to regulatory bodies and the courts, we might be reasonably able to formalize and cope with them. But such, of course, is not the case. Most often, and perhaps most importantly, "the public interest" is a question of political, moral or ethical argument involving not laws or regulations but vital principles.

Thus, President Kennedy asserts that a bill embodying his ideas for financing health care for the aged would "serve the public interest." There is no regulation, no legal dispute, involved here. The President is expressing his own viewpoint; and we must assume that his contention that something is in the public interest does not necessarily make it so. If it *did* make it so, "the public interest" could be established—for once and all—by executive fiat.

In this instance, a majority of the members of the Senate —and very possibly the majority of the American people who had studied the issue—did not consider the bill as drafted to be in the public interest. It was voted down.

Or again, a magazine writer observes that "The President's economic advisers . . . are giving more and more thought these days to the problem of making the public interest felt in the decisions of unions and managements." The writer here, Bernard Nossiter, is using the phrase in a socio-political sense, and his purpose is to inform. But in the process, he appears to presume that the reader has a concept of the phrase that corresponds with his own. This may or may not be the individual case. Opposition has been voiced by both unions and managements to proposed government-supervised "guidelines" over wages and prices. A. H. Raskin, veteran labor writer and member of *The New York Times* editorial board, has suggested that "the public interest" as applied by the White House to its methods in labor disputes is already "confusing" and "unintelligible."

Writing in *The Reporter* of October 11, 1962 (in the May 24 issue of which magazine Mr. Nossiter's article appeared), Mr. Raskin declares:

> The Kennedy administration has been more imaginative than its predecessors in creating tripartite machinery, but the lack of statutory foundation and of clear concepts about what was to be done have hampered recent experiments along these lines. The multiplicity of special commissions and boards to deal with such specific problems as the flight engineers' strike threats or the prospect of a major battle on the railroads brings such an element of improvisation into the handling of labor disputes that neither side is ever certain what settlement formula represents the White House's last word. The "public interest" becomes an elastic yardstick, confusing to the principals and unintelligible to the public.

The need for definition of "the public interest" has been pointedly expressed in another way by Joseph L. Block, chairman of Inland Steel Company. In discussing the relationship between government, labor, and management, Mr. Block said:

> ... Surely the greater good of the nation as a whole should be of paramount importance to everyone and while no one has an omniscient power to define "public interest" accurately at any given time, and certainly not all of the time, it surely behooves all of us—and most particularly government—to endeavor to do so. Failure to do this would seem to me like trying to steer a ship without a compass.

After pondering the thoughts set forth in these preceding pages, I was convinced that the subject warranted further study and I resolved to enlist the aid of others in the task. Fifty leaders in education, government, theology, and labor have been kind enough to give me their considered answers to specific questions. The largest number are in academic fields and many will be recognized as authors of important books and treatises in these fields.

Several members of our firm who are well experienced in opinion study and analysis have joined with me in examining these views. We did not undertake the study as a large-scale, formal research, and the results are not offered as such. But I believe they will be of significant interest, and possibly of value, to anyone faced with the constant and often critical problems of dealing with "public interest" issues.

A sizable body of opinion exists that no precise definition of "the public interest" is possible. Several of those who gave me their thoughts said it could not be defined at all, and about one out of three doubted that any exact meaning could be established.

Dr. Walter G. Muelder, Dean of the Boston University School of Theology, noted—perhaps with tongue in cheek—that "the public interest is about as nebulous as the concept of public relations." His comment almost untracked me at the very outset, for I have often acknowledged that I have never devised or come across a definition of "public relations" that was satisfactory to me.

I should add that Dr. Muelder did suggest that the public interest is "roughly identifiable with the common good or the general welfare," and went on to make some pithy observations that are noted later.

Many other views could be summed up by the response of Dr. Peter F. Drucker, New York University Professor of Management and writer on economics and business subjects. Dr. Drucker said he doubted that the phrase is definable, but that neither is the term *life*. "The 'public interest' exists, however," he added, "as an ill-defined and powerful force."

David McDonald, president, United Steelworkers of America, observing that the public interest "is concerned with everything that affects the public," also described it as "the greatest social force, the greatest motivation, for many of the things people do."

A majority of those who said a definition was possible quoted "the greatest good for the greatest number." But some attached qualifications, the principal one being that the interests of the "minority" must also be protected. As put by Dr. Amos H. Hawley, of the University of Michigan Department of Sociology, the public interest "has to do with a concern for the welfare of the public as a whole, not to exclude the welfare of specific groups or interests where their welfare advancement promises to contribute directly or indirectly to that of the whole."

A. H. Sypher, editor of the *Nation's Business*, said he regards something as being in the public interest "if it is a benefit to the clear majority of the public and has no detrimental effect to the minority or any minority group."

There was no indication that any of these men was necessarily referring to racial or religious minorities, but to any groups of individuals with common interests who might not be a part of "the greatest number." Among such groups might be union members, businessmen, students, military reservists, etc.

A most significant philosophical approach emerged from a number of views that equated "the public interest" with long-range aspirations. Dr. Roswell P. Barnes, executive secretary in the United States of the World Council of Churches, expressed the idea in this manner:

"The paramount public interest is the formulation of sound purposes and the setting of stirring goals. What is it that the public wishes to do? Where is it the public wants to go?"

An excellent phrasing of this premise, I believe, has been contributed by Dr. John A. Vieg to a document prepared by Dr. Wayne A. R. Leys and Dr. Charner Marquis Perry, "Philosophy and the Public Interest." Dr. Vieg states:

> It (the concept of the public interest) will be a reflection of one's dream of a model democratic society. Next, since my own conception of such a society would be marked by growth and development, and not constitute a static condition, the public interest would have to be defined in terms both of fulfillment of the ideal and of progress in its ever finer flowering. To adapt an idea from Edmund Burke, *the public interest requires doing today the things that men of intelligence and good will would wish, five or ten years hence, had been done.* (Italics mine.)

William P. Rogers, former attorney general of the United States, said the public interest "means that which serves the greatest number of people in the best way *over the longest period of time* . . . It is not necessarily synonymous with the most immediate benefits to the citizenry."

Another noteworthy viewpoint was that the concept of

"the public interest" cannot be generalized because it is a personal attitude and must necessarily vary with the individual.

The president of California Institute of Technology, Dr. L. A. DuBridge, commented: "As it is with other terms such as liberty, love, welfare, democracy, it is a term of broad and varied meaning, and a definition which one person might make would probably not be acceptable to most other people."

Dean Earnest S. Brandenburg of University College, Washington University of St. Louis, said:

> It should be remembered that this is always a subjective judgment. Any definition of "public interest" will be made by a human being who may (probably will) omit or overemphasize some element; moreover, when this definition is applied by him or someone else, the same subjective kind of judgment must be made, which means that it is only one person's evaluation—not an incontrovertible "fact."

And Senator John G. Tower, Republican of Texas, brought it down to cases when he observed that "politically my definition would not be the same as John F. Kennedy's."

"Generally," he added, "that which is in the public interest promotes the general welfare, well-being, and security of the citizenry. All would agree to that but where we differ is in the idea of what 'promotes.' "

There were comments, also, that many persons, including some in government, think of "the public interest" only as something in competition with "the private interest."

Senator Eugene J. McCarthy, Democrat of Minnesota, told us that he does not use the phrase, "the public interest," and objects to those who *do* use it in congressional debates. Senator McCarthy said:

I prefer to use an older term, but one which people understand—"common good." Often "the public interest" is used as an opposite of "the private interest," thereby passing word judgment against "private interest." This is a false contract in debates and gives a false impression. The term "public interest" is a self-service term, by which the user implies that those who disagree on a particular matter are automatically opposed to what is in the "public interest."

What are the criteria that determine what is in the public interest?

Again, there is no simple answer here, unless you are willing to consider one succinct response: "In times of stability, politics. In times of chaos, brute force."

The ideas are wide-ranging and varied. In large part, they tend to resolve into a set of basic questions. How many people will be affected? How many people will be benefited? How many will be harmed? How significant are the effects going to be? What are the probable long-range results?

The concern with effects both on and by "minorities" is evident in many views on criteria. Dr. Alexander De Conde, professor of history at the University of California, takes both aspects into account in his suggestions:

> Does a policy or action serve the welfare of the majority without inflicting grievous injury on a minority?
>
> Does it advance the welfare of the nation, and, if possible, of mankind in general?
>
> If such action serves only the interests of a small minority at the expense of the majority, I would say that the action would not be in the public interest.

Indices based more directly on social and economic specifics are found in the views of several. Dr. Hawley refers to "Whatever enlarges opportunity for intellectual, moral and economic betterment of the public, e.g., reduction of wasteful competition, equalization of opportunity, expansion of resources for maximizing opportunity, elimination of invidious distinctions."

Are the criteria constant over the long range, or can they change with changing circumstances? Opinion on this point is almost evenly divided.

A number of views are to the effect that the criteria change with changing knowledge, historical developments, and "the changing weight of various groups." Dean David W. Robinson of Emory University observes that "Because the public is dynamic, so also is the public interest."

Some feel that certain criteria remain durable or "basic" but that other standards may vary in emphasis and change. It is suggested that "established ethical, aesthetic or other principles may remain essentially constant." Dr. Emory S. Bogardus, editor of the *Journal of Sociology and Social Research*, asserts that "In fundamentals they do not change, that is, relating to human needs, but in particular expressions they may change." Mr. Allen King, director of social studies, Cleveland Board of Education, believes: "The paramount long-range public interest probably remains quite constant, but the short-range public interest may properly lead to varying emphasis upon the several elements of the public interest, e.g., periods of peace and war may change the relative emphasis upon freedom and security."

Who is best qualified to judge what is in the public interest?

This perhaps is the key question. It is also, according to a number of those who devoted thought to it, the most difficult to answer. Such initial reactions as "this is the critical question," "it is very difficult to say," and "this is not a simple question to undertake" were common.

Nevertheless, the responses in large part were—as might

have been expected—acutely thoughtful and, I believe, revealing and useful.

One-half of the total opinions conclude that *the people* are best qualified to judge. There are, of course, many varying interpretations of the implications of "the people," and the role of the people in the judgment is at times referred to as "ultimate" and "final."

The president of the United Steelworkers of America, Mr. McDonald, tells us: "This is a chief area not so often thought of . . . No one can be the sole judge of what is in the public interest. The final judge, of course, is the people."

Mr. Rogers, whose profession is the law, does not suggest that it is primarily a matter of law—but rather that the people decide. He declares:

> If you believe in democracy and in democratic principles, it has to be the public—the general conclusion of the people . . . In the long run, the people of this country have to be the judge of what is in the public interest—there is nothing in this nation that cannot be changed by the people, including the Constitution of the United States.

The public as judge, some believe, must be qualified on the basis of educational aptitude. Dean E. W. McDiarmid of the University of Minnesota adds: ". . . assuming of course widespread *communication* and education."

Dr. Ryland Crary, professor of education, University of Pittsburgh, specifies: "Each member of the public—but only if public education is universal and truly effective." Then he observes: "At any rate, it is the only assumption which gives the public interest half a chance."

Dr. Barnes said the question of "who determines" perplexed him. Then he said:

> The people themselves are the best judge. We think of "best" in two ways: best in the sense of competence; best

> in terms of human rights. A man may not always be competent to judge, but he is always a human being. As such, he has the right to decide whether something is or is not in the public interest—his interest.
>
> Of course, in a country like this people do not judge directly; they do not always judge at all. They delegate their responsibility to judge to the persons who deal in public affairs.

But he added:

> Our founders waited for no man. They defined our purposes, chose our goals and resolutely fought for them. They did not expect, did not want, government to define goals or impose them. It is dangerous to think that government is the totality of public interest.

Only two responses were unreserved to the extent of that of Senator McCarthy, who states: "Under the Constitution, the decision is made that the President and the two Houses of the Congress are best qualified as to national issues. This is one of the responsibilities that go with the office. Whether we are best qualified or not, these have been the procedures set up."

H. L. Forkner, Jr., managing editor of the Bureau of Publications at Teachers College, Columbia University, declares that: "The people themselves" are best qualified "through the voice of their elected officials and representatives . . . In fact, by definition, no one else is fit to judge."

It is perhaps most significant that the President was specifically named by only three as being best qualified to judge what is in the public interest. In addition to Senator McCarthy, Dr. Arthur Upgren of Macalester College specified the President and the Congress, and added the Supreme Court. Dr. Richard Lester, professor of economics, Princeton

University, said: "Probably the President of the United States."

Article 2 of the Constitution, dealing with the Executive Branch, devotes only 320 words to designation of the duties and powers of the President. It is interesting that these words contain no reference to "public interest," "national interest," "common good" or any similar phrase. Of course, the Preamble to the Constitution expresses the purpose of "We, the people" to "promote the general welfare," and the inference of implementation of this aim by the President may be made.

Perhaps this question is put into perspective by Dr. Hawley who, believing that determination is "the responsibility of the public," suggests that "it should be the outcome of discussion and debate, i.e., the political process."

"Leadership is required, not to impose conclusions, but to provoke and lead the discussions."

And Mr. Kenneth E. Boulding, coordinator of the Center for Research on Conflict Resolution, observes:

> The established government is most responsible for the public interest, but this unfortunately does not always mean that it is best qualified to judge. New views as to what constitutes the public interest frequently emerge from philosophers and even from preachers. The process of judging the public interest is a very complex one which cannot be assigned to any one group.

A sizable group of the opinions suggests that the best qualified to judge are those who have the capacity for what has been termed "representative leadership."

Rabbi Jacob Goldberg of New York City would include "government officials, social scientists, clergymen and artists."

Dr. E. G. Homrighausen, Dean of the Princeton Theological Seminary, would nominate "the best minds in the various areas of public life." Dr. Neil Chamberlain, professor of economics, Yale University, designates "those who can best appraise prevailing or emerging expectations free of the common failing of projecting these according to their own private interest."

Qualification in terms of ability to look to the future also is emphasized by others. Dr. David Riesman of Harvard University says:

> Various people are more or less qualified and disqualified: what we need are prophets of which there are not many; politicians may also be prophets; so may intellectuals; sometimes the mass media serve this function, sometimes obviously not.

To conclude these thoughts on the question of who is best qualified to judge the public interest, I would quote Bishop James A. Pike of San Francisco, who replies:

> Almighty God; but because what He might speak to us comes from given individuals, and individuals are rarely free from their own biases or aims, there is no way of having an infallible judgment as to this question. Interpreting certain statutes and administrative orders, the courts have the unescapable responsibility of making judgments in this realm. And, each of us, according to conscience, must take this factor into account in our process of decision-making. What the courts and/or administrative agencies decide may not always accord with individual conscience or opinion. Thus, it is not surprising that there is sometimes public contention in this field and appeals from official rulings.

Can responsibility to the public interest apply unilaterally to a particular group, or does it apply to everyone at all times?

The largest number of views held that it applies to everyone at all times. Half as many felt that in general the responsibility applies to everyone but that it may rest more heavily on specific groups or persons. One-sixth as many thought it could, and often does, relate unilaterally to one group.

A point stressed by several is that responsibility goes with power. "Responsibility varies with power," in the view of Dr. Theodore Kreps, professor of business economics at Stanford University. Dr. Kreps asserts:

> The President of the United States has an overriding responsibility to the public interest. So do the presidents of other power groups such as our giant corporations and trade unions, and governors of States. The voter has the responsibility to try to be informed and to vote, not as he is urged and pushed, but as he thinks. The greater the power and wealth one has, the greater his responsibility to the public interest, which is something far larger than stockholders or bondholders.

Is it ever possible for two groups that are in conflict—management and a union, for example—to be acting in the public interest at the same time?

Four out of five of those to whom this question was addressed answered in the affirmative. The reason given by many is that conflict may produce compromise, clarification, resolution or truth—or any combination of these—that could benefit the public interest. Dr. Riesman says: "The very conflict may be in the public interest, clarifying issues and bringing out themes that would otherwise go unrecognized."

Mr. King believes "the public interest is frequently clarified in the welter of competing ideas."

Dr. Walter A. Anderson, Dean of the School of Education, New York University, feels that "two groups in conflict result in a toning down of the more radical elements, and you get a better solution than if either group had its way."

Dean Muelder of the Boston University School of Theology observes: "Their interests are different and always will be different to some extent. In a pluralistic society conflict of interest is inevitable. There can be no static resolution of the industrial conflict. Both management and union are answerable to the criteria of a responsible society."

Rabbi Goldberg states that "for the free interplay of forces to be brought to bear, each group must represent its own best interests."

The steelworkers president, Mr. McDonald, has this to say:

> The fact that people might appear to be in conflict does not mean that they are not both acting in the public interest. All are motivated by what they think and by what their impression of the public interest is. In matters involving the public interest, each party may be interested primarily in a different segment of the whole.
>
> It certainly is possible for two groups to be in conflict and both to be acting in the public interest. What could better epitomize this than our Joint Human Relations Research Committee in the steel industry now?

This Committee, initiated in 1960, is comprised of five union and five industry representatives. Its function is to meet frequently to explore problem areas of mutual concern. It does not make operating decisions, but does report and recommend its agreements and conclusions. It has the important advantage of permitting the discussion of basic problems away from the economic debates, tensions, and pressures of the bargaining table.

Mr. Boulding presents the viewpoint that "the public interest often lies more in the method of conducting the conflict than in the conflict itself, and a good deal of public policy consists of deciding what are legitimate forms of conflict."

Senator Tower comments: "Using management and labor

as an example, it is possible that the public interest might lie somewhere in between . . . Some think that if it is good for management, it is bad for labor and vice versa while the contrary is true. When business is good and management is happy, the working man is the first to reap the benefit."

While many opinions were related to the management-labor reference in the question, a number of others suggested other examples of fields in which conflict could be beneficial to the public interest.

Other examples mentioned include:

> Admiral Rickover wishes education for the gifted; others wish educational opportunity for all. Both points of view represent "the public interest."
>
> . . . Opposing lawyers in a courtroom or candidates running for election on platforms representing different philosophies.
>
> . . . The recent "prayer" decision of the Supreme Court.

Of those who say "no, it is not possible," Robert U. Brown, editor of *Editor & Publisher*, tells us: "Each side may *believe* it is acting in the public interest. I don't believe that both can do so at the same time. If this were the case, there would be no conflict."

Dean McDiarmid answers the question: "Certainly they can be acting for the interest of their group, their public; but in two diametrically opposed positions, one must always be in the public interest and one not, even though it may not be readily apparent which is which."

How important is the public interest in influencing major political and economic decisions?

With but one or two exceptions, the belief is expressed that the public interest *should* be highly important in the reaching of such decisions. Many, however, feel that its influence does not always apply, and there are numerous qualifications as to the nature, extent or result of its application.

In considerable part, the thought is stated that most major political and economic decisions are reached with an eye to what the decision-makers *consider* to be in the public interest. Some feel that, where the influence appears to be inadequate, the fault may lie with a non-informed public. It is suggested that the process of education and the free flow of information are vital.

Dean Homrighausen says:

> Everything depends upon the intelligence of the public interest. A public interest can be infused with mass hysteria. Then leadership has to withstand the public interest, even though it may mean quite a battle. I think it is most important that public interest be informed and that it bring its judgment to bear.

Dean Anderson responds:

> A politician tries to find out what the public believes. He will vote for programs if the public will support him. It is most important that the public or the publics keep their elected representative informed. Too often a representative's publics are not informed. Education is the key here.

Dr. I. James Quillen, professor of education, Stanford University, says: "If the public is concerned and well informed the influence of the public interest can be very important. Often the public is not."

Several views note that, as put by the editor of *Nation's Business*, Mr. Sypher: "The public interest element in economic decisions is, or should be, exercised through the normal workings of a free economy." Dr. Howard H. Cummings of the National Council for the Social Studies, says: "I am not sure about economic decisions but I believe that, in a market-directed economy, voting at the cash register may tend to give people what they want."

A number of the responses to these questions contain varying degrees of reservations. Dr. Bogardus asserts:

> Actually it is given more lip service than a careful searching out by some politicians, some management leaders, some labor union leaders; but statesmanlike leaders in government, in business, and in labor make the public interest a dominant factor in their decisions.

And several opinions are expressed that the public interest is important in influencing these decisions in the long run but often is ineffective short-range: "It may often be neutralized or subverted by considerations of the moment"—"In the short run, powerful special interests sometimes prevail"—"It may get lost in the pulling and hauling in connection with a particular action or piece of legislation."

Dr. Barnes believes this question gives rise to serious concern:

> The public interest ought to be paramount, but special groups—there is a similarity here with the kinds that weakened France in the Thirties—have taken over. They purport to speak for the public interest. Some speak wholly in self interest. It is this fragmentation that is silencing and steadily strangling the public interest.
>
> I see little evidence of the public interest being given substance and meaning by an enlightened public. Instead, I see a prevalence of looking out for "Old Number One." It seems obvious to me that the public interest is not strong enough to triumph over man's selfish acquisitive attitude.
>
> Believe me, I am not nearly so concerned over the danger of a frontal attack by communism as I am by the threat that a weary and disillusioned America will turn to authoritarian controls.

The thoughts and viewpoints expressed in this study, I believe, are more than interesting; they are highly stimulating and provocative to anyone who considers the public interest an important force.

A statistical summary in itself would have little meaning. Neither would I undertake to offer a set of neat and categorical findings.

But I do believe that some general points can be drawn that may be helpful when questions of "the public interest" are involved in public relations policy and action.

These are presented in the chapter that follows.

19

Study the Issue

THE foregoing chapter, I believe, indicates a wide acceptance of "the public interest" as a powerful factor in the resolution of political, social, and economic issues.

At the same time, we have no established definition of "the public interest" that can assure us it will mean the same thing to a majority of the people who read or hear it in a given context. Decision as to what is in the public interest apparently is one of the more subjective judgments of the individual citizen which he forms at his own deliberate pace. He is not apt to be greatly affected when the phrase is thrown at him simply as a rallying cry.

We must conclude, then, that when we argue for or against something "in the public interest" we must do more than make reference to the term. We must explain specifically and clearly what we consider the public interest to be in this instance. If we are to be persuasive, either the concept we present must approximate that of the intended audience or we must win the agreement of the audience that our concept is the more valid.

The courts and regulatory commissions can make binding

determinations based on "the public interest" as they see it. But they can seldom be content to quote "the public interest" and let it go at that. For them, too, public understanding is important. As we have noted, ICC Chairman Murphy has pointed out that "subjectivity and discretion" are essential characteristics of this administrative process and he suggests that better public knowledge of the process is much to be desired. He declares: "A sympathetic understanding of the commission's aims and purposes, and difficulties faced, needs to be brought home to the general public. Cordial public relations are an end much to be sought after."

It is important to debunk the notion that such legal and regulatory decisions inevitably pit the "public interest" against "private interest." Often private interest—that is, as it may represent the efforts or goals of a specific group or even an individual—is judged to be in support of the best interest of the public as a whole. Many court rulings have borne out this fact.

We have reason to believe that most people do not accept the proposition that the public interest and private interest are opposites—that anything in the private interest is automatically opposed to the public interest. In our study, Senator McCarthy asserted that this misuse of the concept of "the public interest" as appositive to "the private interest" was so repugnant to him that he does not use the phrase and objects to those who do use it in congressional debates.

A particular point I would make is that citizens—businessmen, farmers, professional people, etc.—who may represent so-called private interests need not tolerate the implication that their views are opposed to the public interest on an issue under debate. If they can show that the actions and goals they advocate are favorable to public progress and aspirations, they can be reasonably confident that the minds of most people will be receptive.

In the far more numerous matters involving principles rather than legal judgments, the study very greatly strengthens the premise that no one person, and no one group, is entitled to determine arbitrarily what is in the public interest.

As we noted, only three of those who discussed this subject suggested that the President of the United States was best qualified to judge. He can urge the consent of the governed by asserting that what he is advocating is in the public interest, but he cannot expect that this pronouncement will be accepted without question by the people. There are those who contend that the present administration does seek to use "the public interest" in a proprietary manner. M. R. Lefkoe in his article on this subject has asserted: "The President and members of his administration use it [the public interest] constantly; they seem to take it for granted that their listeners know what they mean by the term, so that no definition is required."

But it is not only government spokesmen, including the President, who need to recognize that they must define their terms when they argue the public interest. In many issues involving claims to the public interest, neither contending party is governmental. As we noted in the study, management and labor are prime examples. It is clear that in these instances, also, neither party is likely to convince people that its position best serves the public interest simply by making the claim. In fact, we have found that men who may be regarded as leaders of public thought are inclined to feel that labor-management conflict in itself can work for the public interest. ("The very conflict may be in the public interest, clarifying issues and bringing out themes that would otherwise go unrecognized.")

Therefore, if management is to prove its case in such conflict, or perhaps even to prove that a conflict that shuts down plants and cuts off employee wages is *not* in the public interest, it must be prepared to emphasize criteria by which it contends "the public interest" should be gauged by the public.

This may mean, for instance, pointing out that protection of the functions of a minority group can be in the public interest. The nation's doctors, who are a minority in numbers, may stress—as they have—that keeping the medical profession free from rigid government supervision is in the long-range interest of the vast majority of the public.

Businessmen, too, are a minority group. And when there is talk of civil rights as being in the public interest, businessmen can point out that they also have civil rights that should be protected. Among those rights, we assume, should be freedom from government intimidation and coercion in the legitimate conduct of their business and protection against conspiracy by politically and economically powerful monopoly forces to destroy their business. Here again, the basic contention is that the buoyant growth of free enterprise is vital to the long-range preservation of the free society as we in the U.S. know it.

The long-range consideration would appear to be important in almost any "public interest" discussion. It would be well to keep in mind the criterion proposed by Dr. Vieg that: "The public interest requires doing today the things that men of intelligence and good will would wish, five or ten years hence, had been done." Had this standard, inexact as it is, been applied to many steps that were held to be "in the public interest" in the late forties and fifties, we might not have been looking back, at the turn into the sixties, at an inflationary spiral that has adversely affected our economic progress ever since.

Another implication of Dr. Vieg's statement that is significant is his reference to "men of intelligence." In appealing to the public interest, we are likely to find it especially important to address the case to those communities of citizens who represent, as suggested by one of our respondents in the study, "the best minds in the various areas of public life." It is they, with their leadership capacities, who often can best grasp that which is most important in long-range terms and help to clarify the issues for all who will make the ultimate decision on them.

Finally, the study has underscored a viewpoint that I have long and firmly held. It is that the public itself can serve its own best interests only if it is an informed public. We may believe that most major political and economic decisions are reached with an eye to what the decision-makers consider to be in the public interest. It is to their own self-interest to make it so. But where the public is either poorly informed on the issue or not informed at all, the influence upon the decision-makers can be either valueless or, worse, misleading and dangerous.

A public well informed on the role of education in our society is more apt to support principles and objectives that professional educators say are vital to our future. A public more knowledgeable in world affairs is likely to give a better hearing to government requests for authority to revise trade policies. Greater public understanding of the private enterprise system can help business to show more successfully the part that adequate profits must play in expanding employment, raising standards of living, and promoting economic growth.

Those who would appeal to "the public interest," in short, are well advised to exert continuing efforts to provide a background of public information against which the public decision can be made.

This subject obviously should not be oversimplified. But I believe that these general suggestions may be made to anyone who would invoke "the public interest" in seeking public support.

1. Study your issue and never fail to explain *why* your position or proposal is in the public interest.

2. Do not use the term loosely or too briefly with the assumption that your authority for it will be automatically accepted.

3. Keep in mind not only the current effects of your position but, perhaps more importantly, its long-term ramifications.

4. Remember that the better informed that people are, the more capable they are of judging where the public interest lies.

Overall, I believe we shall find that "the public interest" evolves from the properly combined energies and principles of all positive elements of our society. Roger Blough, in the conclusion of the January 1963, *Look* article on the steel price controversy, put it this way:

> What is the public interest? And who, if anyone, is the rightful custodian of the public interest?
>
> I believe that no one, however wise, however lofty in purpose, can exclusively define the public interest.
>
> I believe that each of us—teacher, minister, Government official, farmer, parent, editor, laborer, business owner, scientist, artist—sees the public interest from a different point of view.
>
> I thoroughly believe that Government officials, and legislators, have a right to define the public interest—as they see it. I think it is also proper for those charged with the management of a company to act with moral courage in what they genuinely consider to be in the best interests of their employers (the owners of the business), the employees and the customers, all of whom are part of the public. This is

true because the operation of that business affects the health and growth of the American economy.

But basically, "the public interest" is the incredibly diverse lawful interest of each of more than 187 million Americans.

20

Conclusion

ONE cannot be long engaged in the field of public relations without realizing that one of the most serious problems confronting business in our times is the lack of adequate communications—communications that bring understanding. The fault lies both with the sender and the receiver—with the sender because too often he is careless, inexpert or lacking in persistence; with the receiver because he is disinterested and inattentive or just plain uneducated.

The truth is, of course, that even the brightest minds are often perplexed by the confusion of economic, political, and social problems that now crowd upon people not only from their local communities and from Washington, but from the world over. In any one of these fields, the average man can hardly be expected to have more than a superficial acquaintance with the massive developments that are affecting his life profoundly.

However, no one can doubt that we would be living in a saner world if the people of America had a better understanding of our economy, the role of profits, and the vital contributions of private enterprise. In a democracy, let us remember, public opinion is the ultimate ruling force. Business began to awaken to this fact in the thirties when it saw the harsh political consequences of its loss of popular favor. It was then that it turned for help to organized public relations.

I say "organized" public relations advisedly. Every business, and for that matter, every activity with public overtones, has public relations whether or not it recognizes the fact, or whether or not it does anything about it. American business had public relations problems long before the Great Depression. But they were not considered, on the whole, particularly pressing ones—and very little executive thought was devoted to them. It is now clear that this was a serious mistake. When the storm of criticism did come, business was almost totally unprepared to make a case in its own defense.

I question whether American business ever again will permit itself to be found so helpless. In organized public relations it has a shield and a spear. It can defend or it can attack as the need may be. But for the most part public relations functions in building and holding goodwill. In its broader sense, public relations serves business by striving for deeper understanding and wider support of our competitive economy. This is a task of tremendous dimensions.

It cannot be too often repeated that public relations has no mystical power to work miracles. What it achieves in any worthwhile sense must be based on integrity, and on sound attitudes, policies and actions at the very top level of management. This makes public relations a management responsibility, and it is so considered by most advanced companies today. The old slogan—if it ever existed—"The public be damned" has given way to the eternal question in the ear of managements, "What will people say?" This is bound to have a good effect upon the conduct of corporate affairs.

Business organizations are aggregations of human beings, some of whom occasionally commit errors or transgressions. To paint all business as the soul of perfection is just as silly as to smear all business for the misdeeds of a few. And, by the same token, all public relations people cannot fairly be judged by those who would "cover up" wrong-doing or in any way mislead the public.

I have seen public relations grow in numbers of people engaged from a mere handful to many thousands. I have seen its services expand from the early days of press relations alone to the present broad scope covering numberless forms of communication and of counseling. I have seen the public relations function shift from an inconspicuous corner behind a packing box to executive offices under the direction of a policy-participating vice president. I have seen small, one-man counseling firms expand into large organizations with worldwide services.

I believe the growth will continue. We are only in the early stages of the development of a sound and solid profession. This growth will be in numbers of workers, surely, but of even more importance will be the emphasis upon better quality of work, and more skill. Above all, public relations for business will develop its power of communications, reaching into the minds and hearts and emotions of people to gain their understanding, goodwill and support, to the extent deserved.

Admittedly this task is monumental because of the widespread economic illiteracy in this country. This illiteracy strikes at the very roots of our American system of capitalism and competitive enterprise. This system has given us our industrial primacy and stands for our individual freedoms. America's strength lies in its democracy. Yet this very democracy carries the seeds of its own destruction. Uninformed and misled, the people can undermine the foundations of their own liberty. One way they can do this is by encouraging political parties to apply political remedies to economic ills. The result is not alleviation of the sickness, but aggravation. In an article in its issue of April, 1963, *Fortune* magazine said:

> The corporate income tax, like many long standing public evils, has assumed the status of a public good, namely, because it is politically sacrosanct. Since nearly all voters are densely ignorant of how this levy really hurts them, they are presumed to be hot for it. Therefore no politician is supposed to run counter to the tax, and therefore those few experts who know it well would be impractical and idealistic to take up arms against it.

The same article quoted Professor William Vickrey of Columbia University as asserting that the combination of corporate, property, and income taxes makes the United States the most "anti-capitalistic nation in the free world." The need is not for abolition of taxation, but for its simplification, and the elimination of punitive levies.

Many students for years have regarded our income tax levies as a drag upon our economic growth. Mathematics prove that all individual income taxes collected over the 50 per cent rate account for only 2 per cent of the total. Political expediency prevents an adequate revision of the old "Soak-the-Rich" rates conjured up by the New Deal thirty years age, although some easing was a possibility in late 1963.

We might say that the people would point the way on

taxes and other economic issues if they but understood the long-term economic and social implications of their choice. And this assumption, I believe, would be correct. We should never cease making every practical effort to advance general economic understanding. But if we are going to be realistic, we must realize that it is not possible to make this a nation of 189 million economists.

Two roadblocks stand in the way. One is the inability or unwillingness of many people to concern themselves with matters beyond their immediate personal interests. The other is that large numbers of individuals and families look receptively to governmental paternalism because they feel overwhelmed and overpowered by economic forces too complex for them to handle on their own.

Private enterprise seeks to preserve a free economy, or as much of it as possible. This can be done only with the support of public opinion. If "educating" the populace in the fine points of economics is enormously difficult, what then can be done and how can public relations help?

Businessmen need to heed the hard lesson that the common man has little objective interest in their problems, their profits or lack of profits, their competitive difficulties, or their tax burdens. He has no interest whatever unless he can be shown how all this affects him, his job, his family, his well-being. "What's in it for me?" asks the common man and it's a fair question that business must learn how to answer. It must be answered, not in terms you would discuss with an economist, but in human terms, with drama and with emotion.

It must be answered in a non-business language that public relations is seeking to master. This is not to deprecate the intelligence of the people but simply to face the truth of human nature. If you would win someone to your point of view, tell him not why it is good for *you*, or good for a third party, but why it is important to *him*.

Who will ever forget the storm that was raised when the then Secretary of Defense Charles E. Wilson said that what was good for General Motors was good for the country? In the sense that he meant it, the statement was true and correct. But the meaning was easily distorted. If he had said that what was good for the pocketbook and security of every citizen was good for General Motors the reaction would have been different.

Not only do top corporate managements need to understand public relations and make it a major responsibility, but they need to understand political life and the ways of government. Industry of course cannot win out in a head-on clash with government, but it can go aggressively to the people, just as a politician does, and win favor and support for policies which can be shown to redound to the benefit of the people. It can likewise seek ways to illustrate to public officeholders the importance of private enterprise in creating the prosperous conditions that build voter satisfaction and confidence.

It has been aptly said that business does not function by Divine Right, but only with the sanction of the people whose attitudes find expression through government. For this reason, enlightened managements of American industry have come to recognize the wisdom of conducting their affairs in ways that merit public approval. They are aware also of the value of communication as the next step in public relations, the aim of which is to build and hold goodwill and to help the business prosper. They know they should make their voices heard, listened to, and believed throughout the land.

Above all, they know that the public relations function must remain flexible and ever ready to adjust to new situations in a world of rapid evolution and bewildering change. Public relations is concerned with public opinion and attitudes. And, as long as we live in a society where freedom of speech prevails and public opinion is the ultimate power, public relations will be an essential and important force.

Index